The Ultimate A to Z
Companion to
1,001 Needlecraft Terms

D0089746

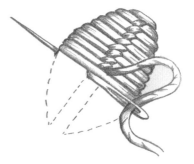

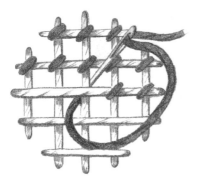

The Ultimate A to Z Companion to 1,001 Needlecraft Terms

Appliqué-Crochet-Embroidery-Knitting-Quilting-Sewing

Marie Clayton

St. Martin's Griffin
New York

www.stmartins.com

Commissioning Editor: Michelle Lo
Design Manager: Gemma Wilson
Designer: Ben Cracknell Studios
Illustrator: Lotte Oldfield
Copy Editor: Sarah Hogett
Assistant Editor: Katie Hudson
Senior Production Controller: Morna McPherson

ISBN 10: 0-312-37777-0
ISBN 13: 978-0-312-37777-9

Library of Congress Cataloging-in-publication Data Available Upon
Request

Reproduction by Mission, Hong Kong
Printed and bound by CT Printing LTD, China

First published in the United Kingdom by Collins & Brown

First U.S. Edition: January 2008

10 9 8 7 6 5 4 3 2 1

Introduction

My grandmother taught me to sew—she had been a dressmaker when she was young, so her standards were high—and my mother taught me to knit. From them I also learned how to reuse fabric and to mend items—the habits of thrift they had learned in wartime died hard. Later I studied needlework at school—it was a choice between sewing and Latin, so there was no contest, really! I often made clothes for myself and for other people, although later the demands of family and work meant that my interest in needlework often had to take second place. Since I find sewing relaxing rather than a chore, I sometimes did a bit of mending or darned socks for fun. Many people thought I was mad: why darn a sock, when you could just go and buy a new pair? Despite this, I was always in demand if a button needed replacing or a hem needed turning up.

When I became a craft editor, one of the great joys was being able to practice old skills again, as well as being able to learn a few new ones. However, I soon found that I now had to look up some terms that I had once understood without question, to be sure of exactly what they meant. New terms for old techniques had been introduced, and some skills that were still perfectly useful seemed to have been forgotten. Hence this book: I decided that I would create a dictionary of needlecrafting terms, which would not only explain exactly what a word meant but would also have diagrams to illustrate many of the techniques. The book covers appliqué, beading, crochet, curtain making, dressmaking, embroidery, feltmaking, knitting, macramé, patchwork, quilting, and tatting, as well as provides general information on fabrics, cloth weaves, and the content of different yarns and threads.

Some terms are used in more than one discipline—and may even mean different things in different crafts. Where this happens, each different meaning is explained. Sometimes techniques, fabrics or terms have different names in the United Kingdom and the United States, so both versions are given, with cross-referencing. I have tried to cover everything as comprehensively as possible—so whatever you need to find, I hope it will be here.

Marie Clayton
Valbonne 2007

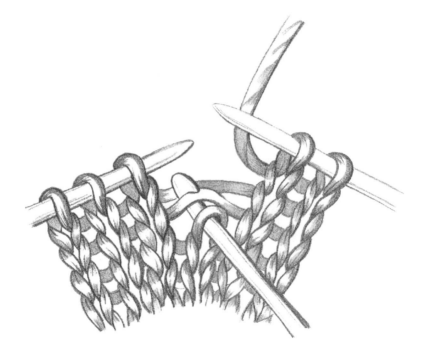

A

abutted seam
A seam used to join non-woven inter-facings, in which the two edges are butted together over a narrow band of lightweight fabric underlay and a line of wide zigzag machine stitching down the join holds the two pieces together. A single line of straight stitching can be added at each side for extra security.

acrylic
A synthetic fabric or yarn made from polymer, which is lightweight, soft and warm with a wool-like feel. It is resistant to moths, oils and chemicals, but is prone to static and pilling.

actual measurement/size
On a pattern, the final dimensions of the finished garment, which may vary from the given "to fit" measurement.

afghan hook
A long hook that looks like a cross between a crochet hook and a knitting needle, used for Afghan or Tunisian crochet.

Afghan crochet
See Tunisian crochet.

aida cloth
Also known as *toile colbert*, fancy oatmeal or java canvas. A fairly coarse, evenweave fabric with a regular grid of well-defined holes, used mainly for cross stitch. It comes with various size holes for different yarn thicknesses, and these are expressed as count. For example, 7-count aida has 7 holes per linear inch. Typical counts are 7, 10, 11, 12 and 14. Aida is made from linen, cotton, or various blends and is quite stiff.

air-erasable marker

A marker pen used in sewing and embroidery to mark lines or motifs on fabric. The lines will disappear within 2–14 days, depending on the fabric and conditions. Some brands allow the marks to be erased immediately with water or made permanent by pressing with an iron, so read the instructions carefully. *See also water-erasable marker.*

album quilt

Also known as autograph, presentation or friendship quilts, album quilts are made to commemorate an event or as a remembrance gift for family or friends moving far away. Generally each square, or block, is worked by one person with a different design, often of relevance to the recipient, and sometimes squares are autographed and/or dated. These squares are then joined together into a quilt. Album quilts were popular in America in the latter half of the 19th century, particularly around Baltimore – hence Baltimore album quilts, which tend to be highly complex, colorful examples with superb workmanship.

ALGERIAN EYE STITCH

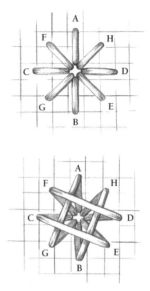

Algerian Eye Stitch

An asterisk-like embroidery stitch with eight stitches of the same length radiating out from a central point. The center end of each stitch is worked into the same hole in the fabric. A variation of this stitch has an additional four stitches from point to point to form a grid over the asterisk. *See also Star Stitch.*

ALGERIAN FILLING STITCH

Algerian Filling Stitch

Used in canvas work, this stitch consists of blocks of three Satin Stitches worked vertically over four threads. The second row is worked two threads up, so forming a staggered pattern that is used to fill large background areas.

alpaca

Natural yarn from the fleece of the alpaca or the fabric made from this yarn. Smaller than the llama, alpacas produce a superb, heavy fleece of fine, strong fiber in a variety of colors, from solid white to black with varying shades and mixes of brown and gray. The luxurious yarn makes wonderfully soft, warm garments and is particularly appreciated by hand-knitters. An annual shearing produces between 1–6 lb (0.8–2.8 kg) of very fine fiber.

Amish quilt

Distinctive quilts made by the Amish, a strict religious group descended from Swiss and Dutch Anabaptists who first settled in North America in the 1720s. Amish quilts use geometric designs and are made in bright, solid colors, often set against a dark background. Traditional designs include: **Bars**, with strips of two or three plain colors alternating within an outer border; **Chinese Coins**, in which the vertical strips are made up of narrow, horizontal bands of color; **Diamond in the Square**, with a square set on point within an outer square; **Nine-patch**, with nine small squares making up each Nine-patch block; **Shoofly**, a variation on Nine-patch in which each corner square is made of two triangles.

anchor

To fix the end of a piece of yarn or thread, or attach a piece of fabric at one point, so that it will not pull away from the main piece. Some stitchers begin sewing with a few small running stitches to anchor the thread, while others prefer to knot the end so that it will not pull through the fabric.

angora
Natural yarn from the fleece of the Angora rabbit or the fabric made from this yarn. Angora is very fine, light and soft and its hollow structure makes it ideal for thermal clothing; research has demonstrated that angora garments are three times warmer than wool ones – although angora is more expensive. In North America the yarn and fabric must be labeled Angora rabbit hair to avoid confusion with yarn from the Angora goat, which is called mohair. *See also* mohair.

Antique Stitch
A form of Satin Stitch in which the stitches are worked on alternate sides of a central line, so that when they are tied down in the middle, they form a raised seam. Also known as Indian Filling Stitch, Janina Stitch, Oriental Stitch or Romanian Stitch.

appliqué
A decorative technique in which a shape or motif is cut from one fabric and applied to another. It is used in quilting, and also to decorate garments and household furnishings.

appliqué block
A quilt block made using appliqué techniques, originally as a way to preserve scraps of expensive or unusual fabric by applying them to a less expensive base fabric. Traditional appliqué designs for quilting blocks

ANTIQUE STITCH

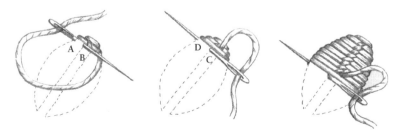

include: **Sunbonnet Sue**, in which the motif is a stylized child with a sunbonnet; **Oak Leaf & Reel**, with four oak leaves set diagonally around the reel so that the stems meet in the middle; **Rose of Sharon,** a flower design often made as a bridal quilt. *See also* broderie perse and reverse appliqué.

Aran
(1) *knitting* A traditional type of knitting, originally used to make sweaters by the inhabitants of Aran, an island off the coast of Ireland. The designs are worked in one solid color—traditionally off-white—but have a rich texture from the use of cables, diamonds, honeycomb stitch, seed (moss) stitch, trellis and ladders. The original Aran sweaters were waterproof, since they were made from untreated sheep's wool still containing natural oils. *See also Guernsey*. (2) *yarn* A natural 100% wool yarn, originally the off-white wool used for Aran sweaters, but now available in a wide range of plain or tweed-mix colors.

Argyle
A knitting pattern of diamonds in a checkerboard pattern, overlaid with a diagonal trellis, traditionally used for socks or golfing sweaters. It is believed to have been derived from the tartan of the clan Campbell in Argyll in Scotland. It is usually created using the intarsia technique.

arm length
The measurement from the shoulder bone to the wrist bone, over a slightly bent elbow to allow room for movement in the finished garment.

Armenian Edging
Decorative stitching for a hemmed edge, worked from left to right with small, even stitches.

armscye
The armhole opening of a garment, into which the sleeve is sewn.

Arrowhead
A triangular decorative stitch, used on tailored garments to reinforce the ends of pockets and pleats. *See also Crow's Foot* (tailoring).

Arrowhead Stitch
An embroidery stitch in which two straight stitches are placed at an angle to each other to form a V-shape. Usually worked in a horizontal or a vertical line.

Assisi work

A counted-thread embroidery technique, in which the design motif is an unstitched area of fabric surrounded by stitching.

asterisk

In knitting and crochet patterns, an asterisk symbol is inserted to mark the beginning of a set of instructions that will later be repeated. Sometimes the end of the sequence is also marked, with a double asterisk.

autograph quilt

See album quilt.

awl

A small sharp pointed tool used in sewing to punch holes for eyelets, or to make belt holes in leather.

B

back

(1) *knitting/crochet/dressmaking/tailoring* The part of the pattern to make the back of a garment. (2) *sewing* To add a separate piece of fabric to the rear of a piece of work, such as a quilt, to conceal all the construction seams.

back width measurement

The measurement across the width of the back at shoulder-blade height, from armhole seam to armhole seam.

backing

The back of a quilt, which can either be a single piece of cloth or pieced. It can even be a separate piece of quilting placed back to back, making the piece a double-sided quilt.

Backstitch

(1) *hand sewing* A row of small, evenly spaced hand stitches, in which the needle enters the fabric at the end of the previous stitch so that the stitches run end to end, as in machine stitching. It is used to create outlines, or the effect of drawn lines, in embroidery work. It also forms the basis of a number of composite stitches, such as Pekinese Stitch, for example. (2) *machine sewing* The reverse stitch on the sewing machine, used to reinforce the stitching at the beginning and end of a seam. (3) *knitting/crochet* Backstitch is often used to join shoulder, side and sleeve seams because it makes a strong join, although it can be bulkier than other stitches. It is worked from the wrong side and it can therefore be difficult to match patterns accurately.

BACKSTITCHED CHAIN STITCH

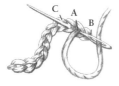

Backstitched Chain Stitch

A composite embroidery stitch, made by combining Chain Stitch and Backstitch to create a firm, textured line. First work the line in Chain Stitch, then work a Backstitch through each chain, either in the same or a contrasting thread.

bagging

Finishing a quilt by sewing the layers together around the edges before turning it right side out through a small opening. This technique eliminates the need for a separate binding around the edges.

balance lines

Lines marked on paper pattern pieces indicating where the lengthwise and crosswise grain of the fabric should fall at key parts of the figure to ensure a good fit. If the pattern pieces are adjusted to fit individual measurements, the relative positions of the balance lines should be retained if the garment is to fit as it should.

Baltimore album

See album quilt.

bar tack

Several short sewn stitches worked parallel and very close together. They are often worked across both lines of stitching at the ends of a buttonhole to reinforce them.

Bargello

(1) *embroidery See* Florentine Stitch.
(2) *quilting* A pieced pattern in which squares of different fabrics are joined in rows, with the different designs or colors stepped up and down alternately.

barré

A fault in woven or knitted fabric, creating an unintentional repetitive pattern of bars or stripes usually running parallel to the crosswise grain. It can be caused by visual differences in the yarn, inconsistent dye, by different structures in the yarn, or by any combination of these.

Basic Couching

See Couching.

Basket Satin/Filling Stitch

Four horizontal and four vertical straight stitches, all of equal length, worked in adjacent blocks and then repeated alternately to give the effect of basket weave when complete.

basketweave needlepoint

A diagonal stitch that crosses over the intersection of a vertical and horizontal thread of a needlepoint canvas. Each succeeding and adjacent stitch is then placed in a diagonal row, rather than horizontally or vertically. At the end of each diagonal row, the stitching is reversed. Also known as Basketweave Tent Stitch.

BASQUE STITCH

Basque Stitch

A looped stitch with a twist, in which the needle comes up through the fabric, in again slightly to one side of this point, and then takes a small stitch downwards from here, with the working end of the thread forming a reversed "S" around the needle. Then a small tying stitch is brought over the bottom of the loop and the needle brought up ready for the next stitch.

basting
A technique used to temporarily hold layers of fabric together for fitting or to stop them slipping as seams are stitched. It is traditionally done with large, single-thread stitches, but—particularly in quilting—can also be done with pins, safety pins, basting spray, or plastic ties from a basting gun.

basting thread
A strong, plain thread used for basting. It is available in a limited range of colors, as it is not meant to be permanent. Ordinary sewing thread can also be used.

batik
Traditional Indonesian fabric, in which designs are painted on fabric in hot wax and the fabric is then dyed. The parts covered in wax resist the dye and remain the original color; this process can be repeated several times using different colors to make richly complex and colorful designs.

batiste
A lightweight, fine, sheer fabric in a plain weave, made of cotton, linen, silk, or blended fibers. It has an excellent drape, gathers beautifully and is often mercerized to add shine. It is used for clothing, particularly blouses, baby clothes, and handkerchiefs.

batting
The middle layer of a quilt, lying between the top and the backing. It is traditionally made of cotton fibers or wool, and in antique quilts could be an old blanket or worn-out quilt. It is now generally a processed felted material that can be purchased pre-cut or by the length from a roll, and is normally cotton, polyester or a blend of the two. Wool and silk batting is available by special order.

Bead Edging Stitch
This embroidery stitch resembles braid and is often used to create a border. It is a knotted stitch that is worked from left to right. Also known as Rosette Chain Stitch.

Embroidery Note
If one were to study collections of embroidery work in museums, exhibits, personal and commercial sources, one could record over 300 types of stitches used.

BEADED STITCH

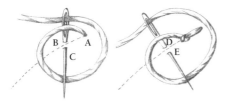

Beaded Stitch

A straight stitch with a knot at the end. It is used mainly for outlines, but can be used as a filling stitch by working parallel rows, staggering the position of the knots. Also known as Coral Stitch, German Knot, Knotted Stitch, or Snail Trail.

beading

(1) *jewelery* Making items of jewelery by threading beads onto thread or fine wire. (2) *crochet/knitting* Incorporating beads into a piece of work by bringing one at a time into position while making a stitch. For knitting and crochet all the beads required need to be threaded onto the yarn before work is begun, as more beads can only be added later by cutting the yarn, or unraveling it and threading them on from the other end. (3) *sewing* Adding beads to the surface of fabric by stitching them in place. In sewing, beads can be threaded onto the needle as they are needed. (4) *weaving* Creating a beaded fabric on a loom. The beads are threaded on the warp threads and held in place by the weft threads.

beading mat

A pile mat, sometimes with a raised edge, to prevent loose beads rolling around while working.

beading needle

A long, fine needle with a large, easy-to-thread, flexible eye that collapses flat to go through a small bead hole.

beadstring

A strong, nylon thread specially designed for jewelery, sewn and woven beading. It is non-stretch and easy to knot between beads.

belt carrier

A small loop at the waistline of a dress or pants to hold a belt in position. It can be made of fabric to match the garment, or hand-worked as a chain of thread, or in Blanket Stitch worked over several strands of thread.

Berlin Stitch

See Cross Stitch.

Berwick Stitch

This stitch is similar to Blanket Stitch, but instead of just carrying the thread around the point of the needle it is wound around to form a tight knot. When worked in two rows of stitches going in opposite directions with the knots together, a fishbone pattern is created.

bias

A line on the diagonal of the fabric. True bias is at 45° to the crosswise and lengthwise grains.

bias strip

A strip of fabric cut on a 45° diagonal to the straight grain of a piece of fabric. It is used to bind edges, particularly curved edges. It stretches very easily and should be handled with care.

bias-strip appliqué

There are two different styles of appliqué that use lengths of bias-cut fabric. **Stained-glass appliqué** uses dark-colored bias strips to outline shapes in the design, so creating a look like stained glass. **Celtic appliqué** uses bias strips to create complex spirals and interlaced designs, based on traditional Gaelic patterns from Ireland and Scotland.

Bible & Story

A group of traditional quilts, which show interpretations of biblical stories and folk tales or elaborate scenes of daily life that tell a story.

big stitch quilting

See utility quilting.

bind off

Finishing a piece of knitting by passing the first stitch over the next and so on, until there is only one stitch left on the needle, which has the end of the thread passed through it to complete the work. There are several variations on the method. *See also* picot bind off.

binding

Finishing off the outside edges of a piece of sewing. It can be a strip of fabric cut on the straight or on the bias. Quilts can also be bound by turning the raw edges to the inside of the quilt, or by taking the edge of the backing to the front, or vice versa, to cover the raw edges.

blackwork

A counted-thread embroidery technique in which the stitching is done in black thread on white fabric, often as a substitute for lace. It is also known as

Spanish work and was associated with Catherine of Aragon, who was a skilled needlewoman. *See also* whitework.

BLANKET STITCH

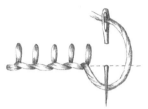

Blanket Stitch

Primarily a border stitch to finish off raw edges, Blanket Stitch can also be used as a decorative feature. The needle goes into the fabric at an even distance from the edge each time, coming out on the edge, and the thread is carried around the point of the needle at each stitch. Blanket Stitch is worked with the vertical stitches set apart from each other; Buttonhole Stitch is formed using exactly the same technique, but the vertical stitches butt up to each other.

blend

A yarn or fabric that is a mixture of two materials, such as polyester/cotton or mohair/wool. The mix may be unequal amounts, such as 50 percent merino wool/33 percent microfiber/12 percent cashmere. The exact composition of a yarn is given on the ball band, while for fabric it is usually given on the end of the bolt.

Blind Hemming Stitch

Hemming Stitch worked under the flap of a hem or behind a facing, so that it is concealed from view. The edge of the hem or facing is rolled back at the stitching point, and the needle picks up one thread from the garment fabric and then another diagonally above from the underside of the hem or facing. It is important not to pull the stitches tight, or a pucker will show on the right side of the fabric. This technique is used for invisible hemming and to hold facings in place.

Blind Herringbone Stitch

Herringbone Stitch worked in the same way as Blind Hemming Stitch, described above. It is useful for heavy or stretch fabrics as the stitches are more flexible than in Hemming Stitch, so they will give slightly.

Blind Knot

See Forbidden Knot.

Blind Stitch
See Pekinese Stitch.

block
To outline the principal sections of a loose cover for an upholstery project on paper or fabric, before the cover is cut in the final fabric. Pattern pieces of a garment are also sometimes blocked before cutting from patterned fabric, to ensure that the design will match across the seams perfectly.

block printing
A traditional form of fabric printing, using wooden blocks. The design is cut in the underside face of the block, which is then dipped in dye and applied to stretched cloth. A registration mark on the block allows for the next repeat to match up, so continuous designs can be printed. Each color in a design needs a separate block; first the outline of the design is completed, then each color in turn. It takes great skill to achieve a good, clear pattern down a length of fabric, particularly when working on multicolor designs.

blocking
The process of pinning out a piece of knitting or crochet to the correct size and shape, before pressing. Blocking is done either on a padded blocking board or on an ironing board, and the piece is pulled into shape and pinned into the board around the edges, using long pins pushed in diagonally. It is usually possible to adjust the size of a piece slightly by stretching or pushing in a little, before steam pressing. The piece should then be left to dry completely before it is removed from the board and made up.

blocks
The basic units that are combined to make up many types of quilt. They are often made from patchwork, but can also be plain or appliquéd. The way the blocks are put together determines the overall design of the quilt.

bobbin lace
Bobbin lace is a delicate fabric worked by hand with many threads, each wound onto a separate bobbin so that its path through the fabric can be controlled. The pattern is marked with pinholes on stiff card and is fastened to a firm pillow, traditionally packed with sawdust or straw. The threads are fixed at the start of the pattern, although more can be added or removed as the work progresses. All

the stitches involve four threads on two pairs of bobbins, which are crossed and twisted to create the stitch. Once the stitches have been made, they are held in position with pins that are pushed through the pinholes into the pillow. Bobbin laces can be worked in two different ways: in **straight laces**, where the motifs and ground of meshes or bars are made in one continuous process; or in **part laces**, where the motifs are made separately and then joined with bars or a mesh ground. The different styles of lace are often named after the place where they were first made, such as Antwerp, Bruges, Brussels, Chantilly, Flanders, Honiton, and Torchon. *See also* needle lace.

bobbins

(1) *lacemaking* The thread spools used in making bobbin lace, which are often turned and carved into complex and beautiful designs. (2) *knitting/crochet* Small plastic shapes used to hold short lengths of yarn, often used to keep different colors separate when working multicolored patterns. (3) *sewing* The small spool for the bottom thread that sits under the stitching plate on a sewing machine.

bobbles

(1) *crochet* A three-dimensional effect, created by increasing and then decreasing in one stitch. *See also* cluster, Popcorn, Puff Stitch. (2) *knitting* A three-dimensional effect often used in Aran patterns, created by increasing and decreasing in one place. (3) *needlecraft* A small wool ball made by winding many lengths of wool around a piece of card, then binding tightly across the middle to secure the lengths before cutting through the looped ends. Also known as pompoms, although these tend to be larger. *See also* pompom.

bodice

The part of a dress between the waist and the neckline, but not including the sleeves.

bodkin

A heavy needle with a blunt point and a large eye, used to thread tape, elastic, ribbon or cord through a casing or heading.

BOKHARA COUCHING

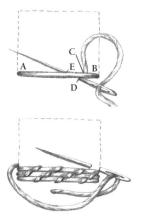

Bokhara Couching

An ornamental stitch for filling in leaves or petals, which has a laid thread with tying stitches set at regular intervals over it, often forming a pattern. The tying stitches are pulled tight, leaving the laid thread slightly loose. In Bokhara Couching, the laid thread and the tying stitches are usually worked with the same thread but they can be worked in contrasting threads. *See also* Couching, Romanian Couching.

bolt

An amount of fabric, wound onto a round tube or a flattened oval cardboard form. The fabric is usually folded lengthwise, right sides together, and the amount in a bolt depends on the type of fabric and the manufacturer. Wholesale fabric stores often sell fabric by the bolt, rather than by cut length.

bonded

Two separate pieces of fabric that have been fused together over their entire area with fusible webbing or a similar adhesive medium.

boning

Narrow strips of plastic or metal inserted into a casing of fabric and used to stiffen sections of a closely fittedgarment to prevent them slipping or rolling—for instance, the bodice of a strapless dress. The name comes from the fact that the strips were originally made of whalebone.

border

(1) *knitting* Strip of design in color or pattern within a plain piece of work.
(2) *sewing* Strips of fabric applied to the edges of a piece of work, creating a frame to hold the design together.

bouclé

A yarn with an uneven thickness,

creating an irregular knobbly effect, or the fabric made from such a yarn.

BOUND BUTTONHOLE

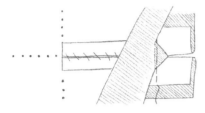

bound buttonhole

A buttonhole edged with narrow strips of fabric, rather than Buttonhole Stitch. Often used on tailored garments.

bound pocket

A bound pocket is made in exactly the same way as a bound buttonhole, but on a larger scale, and the lower binding piece is much deeper so that it continues down to form one side of the pocket. Bound pockets are usually used on tailored garments. *See also* stand pocket.

bound seam

An ordinary seam with each raw edge enclosed, or bound, with a bias binding. This finish is used on fabrics that fray badly, or on the seams of unlined jackets or coats.

boutis quilt

A group of thick, padded wholecloth quilts, which originate from the Mediterranean coastal area around Marseilles.

Box Stitch

(1) *sewing* Four lines of stitching worked in a square or rectangle, sometimes with diagonal crossed lines between the corners. Mainly used to stitch the ends of handles to a bag for a strong join, or to form joints at the knees and elbows of sewn toys. Sometimes referred to as box-stitching. (2) *knots* Alternative name for a Reef or Square Knot.

braid

(1) *needlecraft* A length of cord formed by braiding three strands of yarn or thread. Braid is usually made in one or three colors. (2) *crochet* A narrow length of material made using crochet stitches. A braid is different to an edging, as it has a decorative finish along both edges.

Braid Stitch

See Gordian Knot Stitch.

brick block

Arrangement of rectangular blocks in a quilt, set so that the short side seam of each block in a row falls in the center of the blocks in the rows beneath and above, so the layout looks like a brick wall.

Broad Chain Stitch

See Reverse Chain Stitch.

BROAD STEM STITCH

Broad Stem Stitch

An embroidery stitch in which two vertical rows of diagonal straight stitches are arranged in a V-shape. A row of Backstitch is then worked between the two rows, usually in a contrasting color. *See also* Arrowhead Stitch.

broadcloth

A densely textured 100 percent wool cloth with a plain or twill weave and a lustrous finish. It was used to trade with Native Americans and so also became known as tradecloth. Broadcloth is now often used in North America to describe closely woven silk, cotton, or synthetic fabric with a narrow crosswise rib.

brocade

A heavy, rich fabric with a slightly raised pattern woven on the surface. Traditionally it was made in colored silk, particularly in gold or silver threads.

broderie anglaise

Fine cotton or linen fabric with cutwork embroidery in matching thread, usually in floral patterns. Patterns were originally based on simple eyelets and ovals, but later Satin Stitch elements and different types of cutwork "ladders" were included. Traditionally broderie anglaise was white but it is now available in other colors, usually pastels. Despite the name, which means "English embroidery", its origins are uncertain.

broderie perse

A type of traditional appliqué in which motifs are cut from a patterned fabric and applied in a new pattern to a plain background fabric. The name means "Persian embroidery" and dates from around 1851, but the technique is older. At first Indian chintz, with its complex designs and wide range of colors, was popular for this technique but later some manufacturers printed designs specifically to be cut out and applied in this way.

broomstick lace

Also known as jiffy lace, broomstick lace is an open fabric of crocheted holes, worked on a very large needle called a broomstick or jiffy lace needle, along with a normal crochet hook. Loops are put on the needle in one direction and crocheted off in the other. The size of the broomstick determines the size of each hole in the lace, but the size of hook chosen depends on the yarn being used, not on the size of the needle.

buckram

A coarse, stiff fabric used to give body to items such as belts and baseball cap peaks, and to hold the heading erect in curtains and drapes.

bugle beads

Long, thin tube beads cut from canes of glass, which can also be twisted to form spiral tubes. Some bugle beads have sharp edges that can cut the thread, so check before purchasing.

BULLION STITCH/KNOT

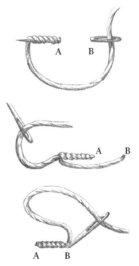

Bullion Stitch/Knot

Also known as Coil Stitch, Grub Knot, Porto Rico Rose, Post Stitch, Worm Stitch. An embroidery stitch in which the thread is coiled around the needle between each stitch to give a corded effect when complete.

burlap

Known as sackcloth in the UK. A loosely constructed, heavy weight, plain-weave fabric used as a carpet backing, and as inexpensive packaging for sacks of grain or rice. In some periods it has also been popular as a drapery fabric.

burnout

A pattern created on fabric by applying a chemical, instead of color, during the printing process. Simulated eyelet effects can be created if the chemical destroys the fiber to create a hole, which can then be over-printed with a simulated embroidery stitch to create the eyelet effect. Burnout effects can also be created on velvets made of blended fibers, in which the ground fabric is left unharmed but the pile is burned away in a brocade-like pattern. This kind of fabric is also known as devoré.

bust

Womens' chest measurement. Take the bust measurement around the fullest part, with the tape slightly higher at the back. Patterns should normally be selected by bust measurement and adjusted elsewhere to fit if necessary. However, if the bust is 4in (10cm) or more bigger than the measurement underneath around the chest, buy patterns one size smaller than the bust measurement and adjust through the bust. This will ensure that the shoulders and armholes are in proportion to the rest of the body and will still retain a good fit.

BUTTERFLY CHAIN STITCH

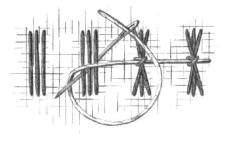

Butterfly Chain Stitch

An embroidery stitch worked in two parts. First, make a foundation row of groups of three vertical straight stitches, spacing the groups about the same width apart as the area covered by the three stitches. Next, bunch together each group of stitches with a twisted chain stitch. This stitch can be worked in two different threads and/or colors.

butting
Bringing two edges together so that they touch but do not overlap.

buttonhole band
Also known as button band. Most often used on knitted or crocheted garments, this is the narrow band of edging that runs from the base to the neckline, and sometimes around the neck and down to the base again in one piece. It can be worked with the garment, added afterwards by picking up stitches and knitting it on, or made separately and stitched on. Along one side it holds the buttons and on the other there are matching buttonholes. Women's garments generally button right over left and men's left over right.

Buttonhole Stitch
Primarily a border stitch to finish off the raw edges of buttonholes, but can also be used as a decorative feature. The needle goes into the fabric at an even distance from the edge each time, coming out on the edge, and the thread is carried around the point of the needle at each stitch. Buttonhole Stitch is worked with the vertical stitches set next to one another; Blanket Stitch is formed using exactly the same technique, but the vertical stitches are set apart from each other. *See also* Blanket Stitch.

Byzantine Stitch
A canvaswork stitch worked diagonally over four or more vertical and horizontal threads. *See also* Florentine Stitch.

cable

A knitting technique in which one group of stitches is crossed over another alternately at regular intervals to create a twisting, rope-like effect. The number of stitches worked can be varied to make wider or narrower cables. Cables and bobbles are the basic techniques for Aran knitting. *See also* cable4back and cable4front.

cable cast on

A method of casting on to begin knitting using two needles, which produces a strong, firm edge with a cable twist along the base. Place a slip knot on the left needle, slide the tip of the right needle upwards into it from front to back, then wind the yarn clockwise around the tip of the right needle. Pull the loop through the slip knot to create a stitch on the right needle, transfer it to the left needle. Continue in this way to create

the required number of stitches. *See also* chain cast on, invisible cast on, long-tail cast on, picot cast on, thumb cast on.

Cable Chain Stitch

An embroidery stitch that creates a neat line of chain. It is worked downwards and makes a pretty border. Start by making one Chain Stitch. Then, instead of taking the needle back through the fabric inside the chain, loop the thread around the tip before beginning the next Chain Stitch with the needle just outside the first chain and directly beneath it.

cable cord

A soft cord, usually made of cotton, used for cording and piping and available in several different sizes.

cable needle

A short, double-pointed knitting needle used when knitting cables, often with a kink in the center to hold the stitches being worked.

CABLE STITCH

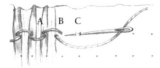

Cable Stitch

Used in smocking, Cable Stitch consists of a double row of evenly spaced running stitches, with the stitch on the upper row centered over the gap between two of the stitches below. *See also* smocking.

cable4back

Notation in a knitting pattern to work four stitches in a cable that twists to the right. On the right side row, work to the position of the cable and then slip the next two stitches onto a cable needle.

Holding these stitches at the back of the work, knit the next two stitches, then the two stitches from the cable needle.

cable4front

Notation in a knitting pattern to work four stitches in a cable that twists to the left. Work as for cable4back, but hold the stitches on the cable needle at the front of the work.

calico

(1) *US* A tightly woven cotton-type fabric with an all-over print, usually a small floral pattern on a contrasting background color. It is commonly used for dresses, aprons and quilts. In the UK, this fabric is known as sprigged cotton.

(2) *UK* Term for a fabric made from unbleached—and often not fully processed—cotton. It is less coarse and thick than canvas or denim, but it is cheap and is often used to make couture garments to test the fit before they are made up in the final expensive fabric. The US term for this fabric is muslin.

calottes

Also called necklace ends, these are tiny clam-shaped pieces of metal that are closed over the knot at the end of a piece of beading thread to conceal it and connect the thread to the necklace clasp. They give a professional-looking finish to hand-made necklaces.

camel hair
Fine, soft and lightweight wool-like fabric made from the fleece of the two-humped Bactrian camel. The fleece is collected as it falls off in clumps in spring. It is used to make outer garments such as coats and is sometimes woven with wool.

canopy
(1) Fabric draped or hung over a frame attached to a four-poster bed. (2) A decorative treatment above a headboard. *See also* tester.

canvas
(1) *embroidery* Needlepoint canvas is available in three different kinds. **Mono canvas** has woven threads and is the most flexible and expensive type. **Interlock canvas** has the warp and weft threads locked together where they intersect and is cheaper, but harder to work as the needle doesn't pull through as easily, especially with heavier threads or metallics. It is sold in various counts, from very large holes for rugs (7 or 8 count) to about 18 count for embroidery. **Plastic canvas** comes in small sheets of various shapes and is good for children to use and for rigid projects like boxes and tags. *See also* penelope canvas, waste canvas. (2) *sewing* A strong, coarse unbleached cloth usually made from hemp or flax and used to make sails, tents, strong bags and work clothes. Also known as sailcloth. *See also* duck.

canvas work
See needlepoint.

carbon transfer pencil
A pencil that can be used to trace over a photocopied or drawn design. The design is then placed drawing side down on a piece of fabric and transferred to it using a warm iron.

carrying yarn
See stranding, weaving.

cashmere
A very fine, soft wool from the overcoat of the long-haired Kashmir goat.

Cashmere Stitch
An embroidery stitch that consists of a series of groups of three diagonal stitches

in slanting rows. The stitching usually starts in the top left-hand corner of the area and the first row is worked downwards to the bottom right-hand corner. The second row is worked upwards, parallel to the first, the third downwards, and so on.

casing

(1) *dressmaking* A hem or tuck through which ribbon, tape or elastic can be threaded. (2) *curtainmaking* The opening across the top of a curtain through which a curtain rod can be threaded.

cast off

UK term, in the US known as bind off. To work a simple cast off, knit the first two stitches and then lift the first stitch over the second. Knit the third stitch, then pass the second stitch over the third. Continue in this way until there is one stitch left on the needle, cut the yarn and pull the end through the last stitch.

catch

To attach one piece of fabric to another, generally with a few tiny backstitches made by hand. For instance, a facing could be attached to a seam allowance.

Centipede Stitch

See Loop Stitch.

center line

A vertical line marking the center/centre of a pattern piece. It is marked on the relevant pieces – usually only the back and the front – and should be transferred to the fabric with an erasable marker, tailor's chalk or a couple of removable stitches.

centered zipper

A method of inserting a zipper commonly used at center back or front of garments when inserting a conventional closed-end zipper. The seam is machine stitched to the point where the zipper should start, with the remaining seam basted in place. Press the seam open and finish any raw edges. Place the closed zipper, face down, centered over the seam on the wrong side and baste in position. On the right side, top stitch across the bottom of the zipper, swivel at the corner and stitch up one side. Repeat on the other side, again working from the base. Remove all the basting stitches.

Chain

(1) *crochet* A series of loops that form

the basis of a piece of crochet, either as a foundation chain, which is the equivalent of casting on in knitting, or as the first stitch of a row or round. Start with a slip knot on the hook, catch the yarn with the hook and pull through the slip knot to make a new loop on the hook—which is the first chain. Continue to make the number of chains specified in the pattern, remembering not to count the original slip knot. (2) *tatting* One of the basic tatting stitches, made up of Double Stitches along a base thread. *See also* Double Stitch.

chain cast on

A method of casting on using a needle and a crochet hook, which gives a neat chain along the bottom edge. The first slip knot is made on the hook, which is held in the right hand, while the needle is held in the left hand. The yarn goes under the needle, the hook goes over the needle to catch the yarn which is pulled through to make a stitch on the needle. Repeat for one less than the required number of stitches, then transfer the last stitch from the crochet hook. *See also* cable cast on, invisible cast on, long-tail cast on, picot cast on, thumb cast on.

chain piecing

A technique of machine piecing in which small units of fabric are joined by running them through the sewing machine one after the other continuously, without lifting the presser foot or breaking the thread.

CHAIN RING

Chain Ring

A length of crochet chain made into a ring by joining the first chain to the last with a Slip Stitch. A Chain Ring is the basis for crochet worked in rounds.

chain selvage

See slipstitch selvage.

Chain Space

The space left between groups of stitches in crochet. When working into a chain space, you are working into the gap left in the row below.

Chain Stitch

One of the basic embroidery stitches, Chain Stitch is commonly used to create lines. It originated in India and Persia, although there it was worked with a fine hook called an *ari* instead of an embroidery needle. It has many variations, including **Lazy Daisy Stitch**, in which the stitches are worked in a circle to create a flower, **Feathered Chain Stitch**, in which the chains are worked in a feather design instead of a straight line, and **Backstitched Chain Stitch**, in which Backstitch is worked through a completed line of chain.

chalk pencil

A pencil with chalk instead of lead, usually with a small stiff brush at the other end. It is used to transfer marks from a pattern to fabric pieces and to mark fabric during cutting or fitting, with the marks brushed away when no longer required.

challis

A soft, lightweight worsted that originated in England in the 1830s and is popular as a fabric for men's ties.

chambray

A cotton fabric that looks like denim but is lightweight. It is a plain-weave fabric with a colored warp and undyed filling yarn. The famous blue working man's shirt is traditionally made of chambray.

channel seam

This type of seam is used as a decorative detail on garments such as skirts and blouses and is suitable for most fabrics. The seam is machine-basted, leaving a long thread, then the stitching is clipped at intervals of around five stitches. Press the seam open, then right side up center it over a strip of the same fabric about 2in (5cm) wide, also right side up. Stitch down each side around ¼–½in (6–12mm) away from the seam line, making sure you catch the seam allowances firmly on both sides. Pull out the machine-basting thread and remove any remaining bits of thread with tweezers.

chart

(1) *knitting* A diagram used in a pattern that gives a representation of the design indicating the placement of different colors. Each square on the chart indicates one stitch and the colors are represented by a symbol, with a key, or by the relevant square being colored in. (2) *crochet* In crochet, patterns for

flat or lacy designs may be expressed as a diagram, with each symbol representing a stitch. Diagrams are also used for filet crochet, but since the patterns are made up of filled blocks and empty spaces they can also be expressed as a grid with squares filled in to indicate a block and left blank for a space.

chenille

A fuzzy yarn with a pile that resembles a furry caterpillar. It is used mainly for decorative fabrics, embroidery, tassels and rugs. Sometimes used broadly to define a fabric woven or knitted from chenille yarn.

Checkered Chain Band

An embroidery stitch worked downward to create a wide border. The chain is worked using two needles, often with contrasting-colored threads. First, create a column of horizontal straight stitches the required width of the border, then thread one needle with a doubled length of dark color thread, and the other with a light color. Each new stitch comes up through the one before and the needles also go over and under alternate straight stitches so the chain is held in place by these; when working the chain, the needles do not go through the fabric. To avoid mistakes as you work, keep the dark thread to the left and the light thread to the right.

CHECKERED CHAIN BAND

chest

Take the chest measurement around the fullest part, with the tape straight across the back.

Chevron Stitch

A simple but effective embroidery stitch that is made up of two diagonal stitches worked in a V-shape, with small horizontal stitches at the top and bottom of each. It can be worked in a single line, or further lines can be worked to make a wide border or an attractive lattice filling. To keep the geometric look, draw guidelines before beginning.

Chiara Stitch

See Double Running Stitch.

chiffon

An extremely light, thin and very sheer fabric usually made of silk, nylon or rayon. It is commonly used for scarves and evening dresses.

Chinese ball button

A small, spherical button made from fabric tubing or round braid and often used in conjunction with frogging. Fasten one end of the tube down and weave a knot as indicated in the diagrams, keeping any seams underneath and being careful not to twist the tube. Pull the ends gently and ease the knot into a ball shape, then fasten the ends very securely to the underside of the ball and trim.

CHINESE BALL BUTTON

Chinese Knot
See Forbidden Knot.

Chinese Stitch
See Pekinese Stitch.

chintz
A glazed cotton fabric often printed with figurative images and large flower designs. The name comes from a Hindu word meaning "sport".

chino
(1) *fabric* A cotton twill fabric used first by the US Army for uniforms but now most often used for casual trousers. (2) *garment* General term for trousers made from cotton twill, usually beige in color.

chunky
A thick, bulky yarn that is thicker than Aran or double knitting/sportweight. It is knitted with large needles and makes up quickly. Also known as bulky.

circular needles
Two short needles joined together with a length of nylon or thin metal cord. They allow you to knit in the round and are also useful instead of ordinary needles when working rows with a large number of stitches. Like plain needles,

they come in a variety of different sizes.

clip
To cut a short distance into a seam allowance or selvage with the point of the scissors. Clipping is done on curved seams, square corners and in similar places, to remove excess fabric so that seams will lie flat when pressed.

CLOSED BUTTONHOLE STITCH

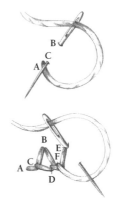

Closed Buttonhole Stitch
In this variation of Buttonhole Stitch, the "legs" are placed diagonally instead of straight so that the stitch forms a row of little triangles sitting on a straight base line. It can be worked as a border or in parallel rows to fill an area.

Closed Feather Stitch

An embroidery stitch that is worked from top to bottom, which creates a wide band that can be used as a border. Draw two parallel lines as guides before beginning, then bring the thread up along one line. Then take a short straight stitch on the opposite line, centered on the point that the yarn springs from, and loop the thread around the end of the needle before pulling through. Repeat on the other side, and so on, in order to create a series of interlocking double loops.

CLOUD FILLING STITCH

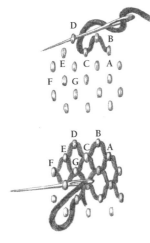

Cloud Filling Stitch

Traditionally used to fill crewelwork motifs, Cloud Filling Stitch is usually worked in two contrasting threads. With the first color, work rows of small, evenly spaced vertical stitches across the area. With the contrasting thread, weave up and down along two adjacent rows, being careful not to pick up the background fabric. Repeat on the next two rows, and so on until the desired area is filled.

cluster

Two or more crochet stitches joined together at the top. Any combination of stitches may be joined into a cluster by leaving the last loop of each temporarily on the hook and taking them all off together at the end. They are used to decrease and add interest to a pattern. *See also* Bobble, Popcorn.

cobweb felt

A type of very fine, open handmade felt that is so thin it is translucent.

Coil Filling Stitch

An embroidery stitch used for filling areas in drawn fabric embroidery. It is worked from right to left; three Satin Stitches are worked over four horizontal threads and between two vertical threads, leaving four threads between each coil. Make a small stitch on the wrong side into the last group of stitches to secure the thread before starting the next row.

Coil Stitch
See Bullion Stitch/Knot.

collar
A band of material set around the neckline of a garment, which can be made in various shapes. *See also* flat collar, mandarin collar, Peter Pan collar, revers collar, rolled collar, shawl collar.

COLONIAL KNOT

Colonial Knot
A variation of the French Knot more suitable for heavier threads. Bring the needle through the fabric just to the left of where the knot is to be. Put the point of the needle under the thread, then take the thread between thumb and forefinger under the back of the needle from right to left, around, and under the front from right to left to form a figure eight on the needle. Take the needle back through the fabric just to the right of where the needle first emerged and tighten the knot as for a French Knot.

colorway
Any of a range of combinations of colors in which a style or design is available.

composition
The percentage of each material from which a yarn or fabric is made. With yarn and thread, this is given on the band or wrapper; with fabric, it is generally on the end of the bolt. It is important to know the composition so that you will know how to treat the finished item when it needs cleaning or pressing.

concealed zipper
A special zipper that is installed so that only the pull tab is visible on the outside. This requires a zipper foot on the sewing machine, as the zipper is applied to the open edges of the seam before it is

stitched. Finish the edges to which the zipper is to be applied, if required, then place the open zipper face down on the right side of the garment with the teeth lined up with the seam line. Pin the tape to the seam allowance, then stitch the seam. *See also* fly front zipper, lapped zipper, separating zipper.

conditioner
A substance to run the thread through before sewing, to make it easier to pull through the fabric and less likely to tangle or knot. Traditionally beeswax or paraffin wax was used, but now many needlecrafters use Thread Heaven, which is specifically designed for this purpose.

congress cloth
A 24-count needlepoint fabric that is a cross between evenweave and canvas, and is particularly suitable for samplers, but is used for all kinds of cross stitch and embroidery. It is mainly white or cream, but is also available in some pastel colors.

continental method
Considered to be the fastest method of knitting. The yarn is held in the left hand, which is also used to move the stitches to the top of the left needle and to control the tension/gauge while the needle in the right hand makes the stitch. Also known as German method.

Continental Tent Stitch
A variation of Tent Stitch where the reverse diagonals are longer than the front diagonals. It is a hard-wearing stitch that is worked back and forth across the canvas or fabric.

CONTINUOUS BOUND PLACKET

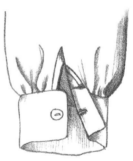

continuous bound placket
With this technique, a narrow strip of fabric is used to bind an opening—for instance, in the sleeve above the cuff. A slash is made in the sleeve at the point above where the cuff will button, then this is opened out to a straight line

and bound with the fabric strip. When the sleeve is back in position, the binding forms a lapped opening. *See also* faced placket, tailored placket.

controlled fullness
The gathering that is required on a long edge so that it can be stitched to a shorter edge.

Coral Knotted Herringbone Stitch
See Tied Herringbone Stitch.

Coral Stitch
See Beaded Stitch.

Cord Stitch
An embroidery stitch in which a line of parallel diagonal stitches is worked with a second line crossing over and slanting the opposite way.

corded quilting
An elegant type of quilting that creates a raised line on the surface of the quilt. A lightweight main fabric is backed with a loosely woven fabric and a pattern is stitched with a double line of running stitch or backstitch to form a channel. A cord is then inserted into the channel, using a blunt tapestry needle. It is only

suitable for straight lines or curving and flowing designs, as the cord cannot be threaded around sharp corners. Also known as Italian quilting. *See also* trapunto.

CORDONNET STITCH VARIATIONS

Cordonnet Stitch
Also known as Whipped or Laced Running Stitch, this embroidery stitch is easy to work in circles and spirals as well as in a straight line. It is worked in two colors—with the first, stitch a simple row of Running Stitch. With the second color, whip in and out of each stitch, going in at the top and out at

the bottom each time. In a variation known as Double Whipped Running Stitch, the second thread is woven in and out instead of whipped, creating rounded loops on either side of the line. When stitched this way, it can also be worked again in the other direction to create a heavier line.

corduroy

A fabric with ridges of pile (cords) running lengthwise. It is available in various weights and weaves and is used widely for both garments and home furnishings.

core-spun yarn

A filament base yarn wrapped with loose fiber that has not been twisted into a yarn. Polyester filament is often wrapped with cotton in order to provide the strength and resiliency of polyester, combined with the moisture-absorbency and good dye qualities of cotton. Core-spun yarn is used for sewing thread and woven into fabrics.

coton à broder

A tightly twisted, mercerized, 3-ply cotton embroidery thread.

cotton

A natural vegetable yarn or fabric made from the soft white fibrous material found around the seeds of the tropical and subtropical cotton plant. Cotton is almost pure cellulose and, in its raw, undyed form, is a light to dark cream, although it may also be brown or green. Cotton fiber lengths vary from less than ½in (12mm) to more than 2in (5cm), with the longer fibers generally being of better quality. Cotton is often classified by its geographical region of origin – hence Egyptian cotton and Indian cotton. **Combed cotton** is made from yarn that has been combed to remove short fibers and straighten longer fibers to create a smoother, finer thread. **Mercerized cotton** has been subjected to a wet finishing process, which results in a stronger, more lustrous yarn that takes dye better to achieve brighter, deeper colors. **Brushed cotton** fabric has been finished with rotating brushes to raise the nap on the surface. **Glazed cotton** has a glossy, polished finish.

cotton lawn

A particularly lightweight, plain-weave cotton fabric.

cotton perlé
A mercerized, non-divisible, twisted cotton embroidery thread.

COUCHING

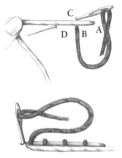

Couching
An ornamental embroidery stitch for filling in areas, which is worked in two threads, one laid on the surface of the fabric and the second forming tying stitches over it at intervals. It is not as dense as Bokhara Couching, in which the laid thread and the tying stitches are usually worked with the same thread. Also known as Basic Couching. *See also* Bokhara Couching, Romanian Couching.

count
The number of warp and weft fabric threads in an inch of fabric. It is used to indicate the fineness or coarseness of a fabric.

counted cross stitch
A technique of cross-stitch embroidery in which a precise number of stitches is needed to complete a design.

counted-thread work
A form of embroidery in which the stitches are worked over a given number of fabric threads.

courses
See rows. *See* also wales.

coverlet
A quilt of only two layers: backing and front, without the batting. Also sometimes used to describe a small quilt for a cot or crib.

Crab Stitch
Single Crochet (UK Double Crochet) worked in reverse from left to right, which causes the stitches to twist for a decorative effect.

crazy patchwork

Patchwork made from random pieces of fabric of all shapes and sizes, pieced together. The seams are usually then embellished with embroidery and the blocks sometimes have embroidered motifs or added buttons, beads or lace for a very rich and colorful effect. *See also* foundation quilting.

crease

A line or mark made on a piece of fabric when it is folded and pressed.

crêpe

A fabric made from a yarn that has been highly twisted before weaving, giving a fine, crinkled effect to both surfaces. It was once made only in black with a dull, flat finish and was worn as a symbol of mourning. It can be made from any kind of fiber.

crêpe de chine

A type of crêpe traditionally made from silk, but now often of a man-made fiber, which is soft, sheer and lustrous.

crêpe-back satin

A satin fabric in which highly twisted yarns are used for the weft and low-twist for the warp and the crinkled crêpe effect is on the reverse of the fabric. If the crêpe effect is the right side of the fabric, it is called satin-back crêpe.

Crested Chain Stitch

Also known as Spanish Coral Stitch, this embroidery stitch is a combination of Chain Stitch and Beaded Stitch. It makes a wide decorative band, or is useful to outline curved motifs. Mark parallel guidelines before starting and work from top to bottom. Make a small Chain Stitch on the right line to start, then make a Beaded Stitch opposite on the left line. Slide the needle under the horizontal stitch you have just made, being careful not to pick up the fabric. Take a stitch along the right line, take the thread around the needle and pull through. Continue in this way to the end.

Embroidery Note

The word Embroidery was first applied to decoratively stitched borders on medieval church vestments. But over time it came to cover all stitched decoration on any textile fabric.

CRETAN STITCH

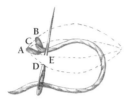

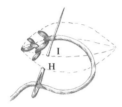

Cretan Stitch

A looped embroidery stitch for filling shapes, this creates a fishbone pattern with stitches caught around each other down a center line. Mark guidelines and work from alternate sides. Also known as Long-armed Feather Stitch, Persian Stitch and Quill Stitch.

crewel wool

A fine 2-ply twisted wool yarn that is used for traditional crewelwork. It is non-divisible but is very fine, so you can work with two different shades in the needle at the same time. Single threads are quite easy to break, so should be worked with care and in short lengths.

crewelwork

A freestyle embroidery technique that is based on the use of crewel wool embroidery threads. On coarser fabrics, you can work the same technique using tapestry wool for a faster result.

crimp bead

Tiny tubes of metal used in jewelry making. They are squeezed tight with pliers onto the wire or beading thread to hold beads in place. They are also sometimes used inside a necklace end instead of a knot.

crochet

A technique of working in yarn using a crochet hook. Crochet can be used to create accessories and garments worked in rows or rounds, or a combination. It can also be worked as shaped motifs that can be joined together in various ways.

crochet hook
A short tool made of aluminium, plastic, wood or bamboo with a hook at one end, available in different sizes and used to work crochet.

cross
Taking one thread over another. The pattern in bobbin lacemaking is created by cross and twist movements of the threads. To work the cross, take the middle two threads of the four and cross the left over the right. The cross is always made this way and never varies.

Cross and Twist Stitch
An embroidery stitch also known as Moss Stitch. Work a basic Cross Stitch first, then a longer vertical stitch that only pierces the fabric at the top and bottom. The twisted stitch in the center is worked around the Cross Stitch threads and should not pick up the background fabric.

cross grain
See crosswise grain.

Cross Stitch
This basic embroidery stitch is found all over the world and is a simple, geometric X-shape that is useful to fill areas or create geometric designs. It is also known as Berlin Stitch, Sampler Stitch, and Point de Marque, and has a host of variations. It can be worked by making a diagonal stitch, then coming down vertically underneath the fabric to work the second diagonal, in which case the reverse shows a series of parallel lines. *See also* Two-sided Cross Stitch, in which alternate stitches are worked before going back over the line to complete the missing stitches, so that both sides of the fabric show the X-shape.

cross3left
Notation in a knitting pattern to work two stitches in a cable that travels diagonally to the left. Work to one stitch before the two cable stitches, slip the next stitch onto a cable needle and leave at the back of the work. Knit the next two stitches from the left-hand needle, then purl the stitch from the cable needle.

cross3right
Notation in a knitting pattern to work two stitches in a cable that travels diagonally to the right. Work as for cross3left, but leave the stitch on the cable needle at the front of the work.

Crossed Buttonhole Stitch

A variation of standard Buttonhole Stitch that is worked with the vertical stitches at an angle, crossing each other in pairs.

CROSSED CORNERS CUSHION STITCH

Crossed Corners Cushion Stitch

Satin Stitch worked in a square, with the stitches sloping from right to left. Then half the square is overstitched in the opposite direction. The next block is worked in the same way but with the stitches sloping the opposite way.

cross grain fold

A fold at a right angle to the grain of a fabric.

crosswise grain

The widthwise grain of the fabric, which runs from selvage to selvage. Also known as cross grain. The lengthwise grain runs the length of a piece of fabric.

crotch depth measurement

To take this measurement, sit on a hard surface and measure from the side of the waist to the chair seat.

crotch length measurement

Measurement from the center back of the waist, between the legs to the center front of the waist.

CROW'S FOOT

Crow's Foot

(1) *tailoring* A triangular decorative stitch, used on tailored garments to reinforce the ends of pockets and pleats. *See also* Arrowhead. (2) *quilting* A stitch used in utility quilting, based on Fly

Stitch, and worked either randomly, in straight lines, or to make meandering "bird's tracks."

cuff

The end part of a sleeve, where the material is turned back or a separate band is sewn on. The cuff can be loose fitting, without an opening, or tight fitting with an opening and a button fastening.

curved blocks

Designs based on curves—either with curved seams or curves created by the way the blocks are put together—have long been popular with quilters. One of the most popular—but most complex to construct—is **Double Wedding Ring**, which is a design made up of interlocking circles. In **Grandmother's Fan** patterns, the block has a quarter of a circle across one corner made up of many pieced segments. Four Fan blocks can be pieced with the fans together to create Dresden Plate. **Drunkard's Path/Robbing Peter to Pay Paul** are composed of square blocks with a circular "bite" in a contrasting color across one corner. These blocks can be pieced in many ways to create a wide range of patterns.

curtain pleats

Even folds in the heading of a curtain. The main types are: **cartridge pleat**—a small round pleat, often in groups of three and usually filled with a rolled piece of stiffening; **French or goblet pleat**—one large rounded pleat, gathered into three pleats at the bottom edge and arranged at intervals, but not creased; **pencil pleat**—a series of even, narrow pleats running continuously close together across the heading; **pinch pleat**—one large pleat divided into two or three and creased the length of the pleat, fanning out at the top.

cutting guide/layout

The diagram given in a paper pattern that shows you how to lay out the pattern pieces on different widths of fabric. It also indicates—usually by shading—which pieces, if any, need to be placed printed side down on the fabric for cutting. Some pieces may need to be placed on a fold line and this will also be clearly indicated on the paper pattern.

cutting line

The outermost solid line on a paper pattern, which indicates exactly where you cut the piece out. Some people cut through the center of this line, while others cut just to the outside of it. It doesn't really matter which of these you choose, as long as you are always consistent.

cutting mat
A flexible mat, ideally with a self-healing surface, to protect the work surface when cutting out pieces of fabric with a rotary cutter.

cutwork
An embroidery technique that involves stitching an outline around areas of the design and then cutting away the fabric inside the stitched line to create an open pattern.

damask

Originally a firm, glossy, jacquard-woven fabric made in China and brought to the Western world by Marco Polo in the 13th century. Damascus was the center of the fabric trade between East and West, hence the name. Damask fabrics are reversible and are characterized by a combination of satin and sateen weaves, so the design motifs have a luster against a matte ground.

Damask Stitch

See Darning Stitch.

darn

To repair a hole in a fabric. Darning can be done by simply pulling the sides of a hole together and oversewing the edges to hold them together. Round holes can have a network of yarn woven over them horizontally and vertically to recreate material to fill the hole. Invisible mending is very detailed darning that is almost imperceptible on the right side of the fabric.

DARNING STITCH

Darning Stitch

An embroidery stitch in which parallel rows of even Running Stitch are worked close together. The stitches can be staggered in blocks, worked diagonally, or offset to create a variety of geometric patterns. Also known as Damask Stitch.

dart

A dart is used to mold the fabric of a garment to the curves of the body. Darts can be straight, for a loose fit, or curved for a tighter fit and they usually start at the seam line and taper to nothing at the tip. Double-pointed darts are used on dresses, jackets and fitted shirts; they are a diamond shape with the widest point at the waist tapering to a point at the bust or shoulder blade and hips. They should be sewn as two darts back to back, working from the center to the point on each one.

decrease
To reduce the number of stitches being worked in knitting or crochet, usually by working two or more stitches together over several rows. *See also* full fashioning.

delica beads
A tubular version of seed beads, which can be used to create an almost seamless beaded fabric with some beading techniques. They are very fine and light, so there are a large quantity in a lightweight packet.

denier
A unit of measurement for fiber, which is also used to define how thick and opaque stockings or tights/pantyhose are. The higher the denier, the thicker the weave and the more opaque the fabric.

denim
A rugged, durable twill cotton fabric that is most popular in indigo blue. Denim is mainly used for casual garments such as jeans, but it has also become popular for home furnishings. Stretch denim has added Lycra.

Detached Chain Stitch
See Lazy Daisy Stitch.

devoré
A type of velvet in which areas of the pile have been removed to leave only the base fabric – usually via a chemical process – to create a translucent pattern against the solid pile areas. It is usually made into scarves or evening wear.

Diamond Star Stitch
An embroidery stitch made up of eight stitches, each going through the same central hole to make a star. The four stitches that make up the horizontal and vertical arms are slightly longer than the four diagonal arms.

DIAMOND STITCH

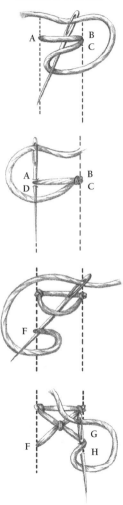

Diamond Stitch

(1) *embroidery* A knotted stitch, Diamond Stitch creates a wide border with the look of trellis. It is worked between two parallel lines and the needle only goes through the fabric along the lines; be careful not to pick up the fabric when creating the knotted cross in the center. (2) *smocking* A trellis stitch worked by taking a small horizontal stitch from left to right on one fold, then another from right to left at a lower level and on the next fold, continuing in this way to the end. Repeat other rows of stitching beneath, each time using alternate folds.

directional stitching

Stitching the seams in the correct direction of the grain, so that the fabric will not stretch as it is being stitched.

distressing

Creating decorative textural effects in fabric by fraying the edges, by melting areas of synthetic fabric, or by pulling the weave apart.

divider pins

Long pins with a large head—often decorative—used in lacemaking to hold the bobbin pairs not in use out of the working area.

dobby

A mechanical attachment on a loom that allows the weaving of small, geometric figures.

doeskin

(1) *leather* A very fine, soft and supple leather made from deerskin or lambskin.
(2) *fabric* A very smooth, lustrous and soft fabric with a fine nap and a compact weave, made of high-quality wool.

Donegal tweed

A plain-weave fabric woven from wool yarns characterized by a random distribution of brightly colored flecks or slubs. It was originally produced as a coarse wool suiting in County Donegal in Ireland.

Dot Stitch

Dot Stitch is an embroidery stitch worked in lines, which can be straight, circular or spirals, or as random dots. It is effectively Running Stitch but is worked as two Backstitches, worked side by side and spaced slightly apart rather than running end to end. Also known as Rice Stitch and Rice Grain Stitch.

dotted Swiss

A sheer, crisp cotton fabric, which is embellished with woven, flocked, or embroidered dots.

Double Coral Stitch

See Thorn and Briar Stitch.

Double Crochet

A type of crochet stitch. To make, bring yarn over hook and insert hook in next stitch to be worked. Bring yarn over hook a second time and pull yarn through stitch. Bring yarn over hook again; pull yarn through two loops on hook. Bring yarn over hook and pull yarn through last two loops on hook. In the UK, it is known as Treble Crochet.

Double Feather Stitch

See Thorn and Briar Stitch.

DOUBLE HALF-HITCH KNOT

Double Half-hitch Knot

A knot used in macramé, also sometimes called Two Half-hitches. Begin by forming a clockwise loop around the vertical string, with the working end on top. Bring the working end through the loop so you have an overhand knot called a Half-hitch. Bring the working end down and to the left, loop it under the string and around through the loop again and tighten to complete the knot.

Double Knot Stitch

See Smyrna Stitch.

Double Pekinese Stitch

See Interlaced Band.

Double Running Stitch

This embroidery stitch looks like Backstitch, but is worked as a row of Running Stitch with a second row worked over the first to fill in all the gaps and create a continuous line. It is best for straight lines; draw guidelines to follow before beginning to sew to keep them straight. Also known as Chiara Stitch, Holbein Stitch, Two-sided Line/Stroke Stitch.

Double Stitch

Tatting is made up of Double Stitches (ds) formed along a base thread. Both hands are used to form the stitch, so it doesn't matter if you are right- or left-handed. When complete, the stitch should slide along the base yarn; if it doesn't, it has not been made correctly. Also called Lark's Head Knot.

double thread canvas

See penelope canvas.

Double Treble

A type of crochet stitch. To make, bring yarn over hook three times, then insert your hook into next stitch. Bring yarn over and pull up a loop. Bring yarn over again and draw through two loops. Repeat three more times to complete stitch. In the UK, it is known as Triple Treble. *See also* Single Crochet, Treble Crochet.

double-stitched seam

This is a narrow seam particularly suitable for sheers and knits, as it prevents the fabric from fraying. Stitch a plain seam first, then stitch a second line within the seam allowance, either in a straight or a zigzag stitch. Trim the seam allowance close to the second line of stitching and press the seam allowances to one side.

DOVE'S EYE

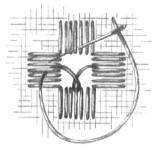

Dove's Eye

An embroidery stitch used in Hardanger. It is composed of four looped stitches, one made on each side of the space left by the cut fabric threads. The stitches are taken under the center Satin Stitch on each side. To complete the last loop, pass the needle under the beginning stitch and insert into the fabric at the other side.

drape

The property of a fabric to fall into folds. If it falls gracefully, it is said to drape well or to have good drape.

drawn-thread work

In drawn-thread embroidery, threads are pulled out from the fabric and the edges of the spaces left are embroidered. Decorative stitches can also be worked over the holes left by withdrawing both warp and weft threads. In drawn-fabric embroidery, the embroidery draws together groups of threads, creating an open pattern in the fabric. The stitches are worked over an even number of fabric threads and the stitching thread is pulled tight with each stitch. No threads are withdrawn, so the final piece is much more durable than with drawn-thread work. *See also* Hardanger.

dress form

A body shape on a stand, which is used to fit garments during construction and can be a set size or adjustable. It may be made from many materials, but it should have a surface that will accept pinning.

dressmaker's pins

Long, fine, sharp pins with a small bead at the end instead of a flat metal circle.

dressmaker's tracing paper

Colored carbon paper usually used with a tracing wheel to trace a shape or pattern markings on to fabric.

drill

A strong, medium- to heavyweight, warp-faced, twill-weave fabric, often cotton. It is used for casual trousers and uniforms.

drop

(1) *curtainmaking* The measurement on a curtain from the top of the heading to the bottom of the hem. (2) *fabric* When loose-woven, knitted or crocheted fabrics stretch out of shape if hung up, pulled by the weight of the fabric itself. Also known as sag.

drop shoulder

A shoulder line that is located below the natural shoulder level.

dropped stitch

A stitch that has fallen off the needle in knitting. If it unravels back for several rows, it creates a run—or ladder effect—in the fabric. Dropped stitches can also be used as a decorative feature.

duck

A strong, heavy, plain or basketweave fabric, available in a variety of weights and qualities. It is similar to canvas, and is usually made from cotton.

duo canvas

An embroidery canvas woven with double threads, creating both wide and narrow spaces, so the effect of two meshes can be created on one canvas by using the large holes for the background and the small holes for detail areas. Also known as double-thread canvas or penelope canvas.

duplicate stitch

Also known as Swiss darning. An embroidery technique made on knitted fabrics, in which the knitted stitch is duplicated in a contrasting yarn so that it looks as if the motif has been knitted into the fabric. It is only worked on Stockinette Stitch.

Durham quilts

A term for a group of quilts made in the northeast English counties of Durham and Northumberland at the end of the 19th century until the First World War. They are quite simple in basic design, but are quilted with very beautiful and complex patterns worked in extremely fine stitching.

Crochet Call
Crochet began as a cottage industry in Ireland with a lace called Irish crochet or guipure lace.

DUTCH STITCH

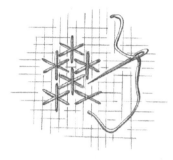

Dutch Stitch

An embroidery stitch forming a six-pointed star. Work the elongated cross stitch first, then work the single vertical stitch. The star shapes can be worked over a large area and should fit together as shown.

dye lot number

Colored yarns are dyed in batches, so a particular color may have a name and/or a shade number—which does not vary—and a dye lot number which changes with each batch. Inevitably the color will vary slightly between batches, so try to buy all the material for a project from one batch. The dye lot number is shown on the ball band.

E

ease

To fit a longer fabric edge to a slightly shorter one by evenly distributing the fabric without creating any definite tucks or gathers. *See also* ease stitching.

ease allowance

The amount added to body measurements to make garments comfortable and to allow for movement.

ease stitching

A dressmaking/tailoring technique for when you need to join a longer piece of fabric to a shorter one. With the machine set on its longest stitch length, stitch a single row close to the seam line, inside the seam allowance. Pin the two pieces of fabric together at the matching notch points, then pull on the bobbin thread to draw up the longer fabric evenly between the two pins. With the stitch length set at normal, sew the seam

with the eased fabric on top to avoid pulling it as you work.

echo quilting

Concentric lines of quilt stitching that follow the shapes of the design.

EDGE STITCHING

edge stitching

To stitch close to a finished edge, seam or fold, either as a decorative feature or to stop a piece of fabric such as a facing from rolling around to the front.

edge-to-edge quilting

Edge-to-edge quilting is a quilting pattern that covers the entire area of a quilt, regardless of the design, or any borders or sashing. The pattern is repeated several times throughout each row. This type of quilting is excellent for quilts that will actually be used rather than displayed.

edging

A narrow band—whether fabric, knitting or crochet—used to border an item. It can be made separately and stitched on, or in knitting and crochet it can be created by picking up edge stitches and working the edging in position. Decorative bought edgings are sometimes also called trim/trimming.

elastane

A stretchy synthetic fiber that is stronger and more durable than rubber. It is smooth, supple and can be stretched over 300 percent without breaking, afterwards returning to its original shape. Its weight and resistance to body oils, perspiration and cosmetics means that it is used for clothing, particularly those items where comfort and fit are important. Also known as spandex or Lycra®.

elastic

(1) A strip of fabric usually containing rubber, so it stretches but will return to its original shape. Elastic comes in white, black and beige and in a range of widths and stretchiness. It is used to gather items in where they need to fit tightly but also to expand for access— such as at waistline or cuffs. (2) The characteristic of stretchiness.

embellish

Adding decorative elements to a finished item.

embroidery floss/thread

There are several different types of thread that are suitable for embroidery, but the most common is made of pure cotton and has six strands that can be divided for finer work. *See also* coton à broder, cotton perlé, crewel wool, flower thread, metallic/metallic-effect/metallized thread, Persian yarn, tapestry yarn.

embroidery hoop

Two thin circles of wood or plastic, the smaller of which is placed under the fabric and the larger over the top to hold the fabric tight for embroidery. The larger circle is often adjustable.

English method

A method of knitting in which the left hand controls the needles and the stitches, leaving the right hand free to move the yarn over the tip of the left needle to form new stitches. The right needle is held tight against the body under the arm and the left needle is held from above, with the thumb and index finger of the left hand controlling the tip of the right needle. This is also known as Scottish method.

English paper piecing

A patchwork technique that involves basting fabric shapes to backing shapes in stiff paper and joining them by hand. It is ideal for shapes with sharp angles or bias seams, as the paper supports the fabric and keeps it in shape. Although the technique is time-consuming, it is the traditional way to assemble many traditional designs, such as Tumbling Blocks, and Grandmother's Flower Garden.

Encroaching Buttonhole Stitch

A version of Buttonhole Stitch worked in rows, with the next row of stitches overlapping the ridge of the row before. It gives a slightly raised effect and can be worked in toning yarns to create shading.

Encroaching Satin Stitch

Even rows of Satin Stitch worked in parallel rows, with each row slightly overlapping the previous one.

entredeux

Two strips of lightweight fabric on either side of a line of tiny eyelet holes. It is used in heirloom work to join two pieces of fabric or to join lace to fabric. The name comes from the French *entre deux*, meaning "between two."

Ermine Stitch

An embroidery stitch used to fill areas, made by making a straight vertical stitch with an elongated cross over it just above the base. The effect is like a six-pointed star, with the three upper arms longer than the three lower ones. It can be worked in rows or dotted randomly.

evenweave

Any fabric with the same number of threads per inch vertically and horizontally, an important feature for accurate count sizes. Most canvases and aida are evenweaves.

eyelet

(1) A small round hole in fabric, which may be hand stitched or created with a punch and lined with a metal ring that grips the fabric on the reverse. Hand-stitched eyelets are edged with overcast stitching or Blanket Stitch to stop the edges from fraying. Eyelets are used for decorative effect, for lacing and in belts.

(2) *knitting* An eyelet increase is the simplest way to increase one stitch when knitting; it leaves a small hole in the knitted fabric, hence the name. Knit to where the extra stitch is required, bring the yarn forward between the needles, then back over the top of the right needle to create a loop of yarn on the needle. Finish the row; on the purl row work the loop as if it is a stitch. An eyelet buttonhole is worked in the same way, but after the loop has been created, the following two stitches are knitted together. The number of stitches on the needle remains the same, but a small hole is created for the button.

EYELET HOLE

Eyelet Hole

A Hardanger embroidery stitch worked over a square of an even number of fabric threads in each direction. One stitch is worked between each fabric thread all around the square, with each stitch going into the same central hole.

eyepin

A blunt pin used in making beaded jewelry, with one end curved into a loop. Eyepins are mainly used for earrings and at the ends of necklaces.

F

faced placket
An opening with the edges meeting rather than overlapping, with a facing usually in matching fabric. Mainly used at the cuff, but sometimes also at the neckline. *See also* continuous bound placket, tailored placket.

facing
A shaped piece of fabric stitched on the seam line of the main garment piece and turned inside to create a finished edge.

Faggoting
A stitch used to join two pieces of fabric, which creates a decorative zigzag effect and allows the pieces to move against each other. Stitch alternately into each edge of the fabric, catching a loop of thread each time. Also known as Twisted Insertion Stitch.

faille
A lustrous, soft, finely ribbed, woven fabric usually made from cotton, rayon, polyester or a blend of fibers. It drapes well and is ideal for evening gowns; it looks like silk taffeta, but is much less expensive.

Fair Isle
A type of colored knitting with rows of small repeating motifs. Traditionally each motif is only in two colors, although there may be far more colors in the overall garment. The yarn not in use is carried across the back of the work until required, creating a double-thickness fabric. Fair Isle is usually worked in Stockinette/Stocking Stitch. *See also* stranding, weaving.

fancy oatmeal
See aida.

fastening off

When working crochet, at the beginning and end of each stitch there should only be one loop on the hook. At the end of a piece, this stitch is fastened off by cutting the yarn and threading the end through the loop, before drawing it tight.

fat quarter

A fat quarter is ¼ yard/meter of fabric, obtained by cutting a yard/meter of fabric in half lengthwise and then in half again widthwise, instead of in four equal strips across the full woven width. It was first available in fabrics for quilting, but is now more widely offered.

faux/fake fur

A man-made fabric with a long "fur" pile, often colored in imitation of an animal's pelt. Fun fur is similar but is made in bright colors and is more obviously artificial. Imitation fur is usually made of acrylic, although other fibers can also be used. It is often made into throws, outerwear, or used as a lining or as a trim on coats or hats.

Feather Stitch

One of the basic embroidery stitches, Feather Stitch was a popular decoration on English smocks. It is worked downwards, making V-shaped stitches that alternate from side to side to create a feathery line. It is also known as Plumage Stitch and Briar Stitch.

featherbone

See boning.

FEATHERED CHAIN STITCH

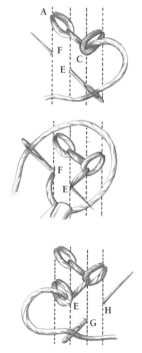

Feathered Chain Stitch

A variation on Feather Stitch, in which chains are worked from side to side instead of a V-shaped stitch. It is worked from top to bottom and is very effective as a border.

feed dogs

The "teeth" under the plate on the sewing machine, which move the fabric along as it is stitched.

felt

Machine-made felt is non-woven fabric made of compressed wool or acrylic fiber and available in a wide range of colors. It does not fray and can be molded to a shape, so it is used for craft projects, to cover game tables and to make hats. Hand-made felt is made from pure wool fleece, which is laid out in a design and then rubbed with warm soapy water to cause the fleece fibers to felt together into a solid mass. Needle felt is also made of wool fleece, but can be made into three-dimensional shapes, such as soft toys. The fleece is roughly shaped and then stabbed repeatedly with a special needle, until the fibers mat together into a solid mass. Knitted fabrics can be felted by being washed at high temperatures and then tumble dried. *See also* cobweb felt, nuno felt.

FERN STITCH

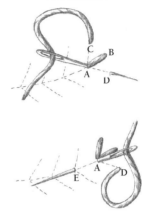

Fern Stitch

An embroidery stitch that creates a delicate, fern-like tracery. It is worked by making three straight stitches angled from a common base, then repeating below with the center stitches running in to one another to create the stem.

fiber/fibre

Natural or manufactured thread or filament from which yarns are spun. Natural fibers include wool, silk and cotton; manufactured fibers include viscose rayon and polyester.

filet crochet

A term dating from the 19th century, when crochet was used to copy lace patterns. The easiest lace to copy in crochet was filet lace, which was worked with a needle and the crochet version of this was named filet crochet. Only two stitches are used in filet crochet: Chain and Single Crochet (US)/Double Crochet (UK). The Chain forms a space and the Single a block, so patterns can easily be plotted out on graph paper and it is simple to make geometric patterns or text.

filling yarn

Another term for the weft threads in woven fabric. *See also* floating yarn.

findings

Small items or tools used when making garments, shoes or jewelery.

fingering

A lightweight yarn, which can be wool, cotton, synthetic, or a blend.

finger-press

To press a fold into a piece of fabric using fingers and a thumbnail.

finish/finishing

(1) *fabric* The surface treatment to a fabric, such as brushing or glazing. (2) *sewing* The techniques to complete a garment, such as stitching on buttons, hemming, pressing. (3) *knitting/crochet* The techniques to complete a garment, such as darning in ends, sewing parts together, stitching on buttons, pressing.

FIR STITCH

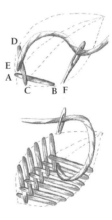

Fir Stitch

An embroidery stitch in which diagonal straight stitches are worked on alternate sides and spaced slightly apart as a filling, crossing in the center to form a leaf vein. The stitch size is graduated to make a leaf shape and they are worked at a shallow angle, unlike Open Fishbone Stitch, which is worked at a more acute angle. Also known as Leaf Stitch.

Fishbone Stitch

An embroidery stitch in which diagonal straight stitches on alternate sides of a central point are worked at quite an acute angle and very close together, crossing slightly in the center. It is worked upwards. *See also* Cord Stitch, Flat Stitch.

flannel

A mediumweight, plain- or twill-weave fabric typically made from cotton, a cotton blend, or wool. It has a very soft hand, and is brushed on both sides to lift the fiber ends and create a soft, furry surface. It was once used for undergarments and sheets, but is now mainly used for shirts and pajamas.

flannelette

A mediumweight, plain-weave fabric, usually made from cotton. It is brushed only on one side and is lighter in weight than flannel. It is mainly used for shirts and pajamas.

flap pocket

Concealed set-in pockets in jackets and coats sometimes have a flap set just above the opening on the outside that covers the access. Tailored garments may have a flap combined with a bound or piped opening—in this case, the flap comes from under the top edging so that it can either be out on display or tucked away inside the pocket. These alternatives are purely for a different visual effect.

flat collar

A flat collar lies flat against the garment to which it is attached. In this type of collar, the curve at the neck edges of the garment and the collar will be almost exactly the same. *See also* mandarin collar, Peter Pan collar, revers rolled collar, shawl collar.

Flat Stitch

An embroidery stitch in which slightly slanting straight stitches on alternate sides of a central point are worked very close together, crossing slightly in the center. It is worked upwards. It is very similar to Fishbone Stitch but worked at a much less acute angle. *See also* Cord Stitch, Fishbone Stitch.

flat fell seam

This type of seam is often used on menswear, sportswear and reversible garments. With wrong sides together, stitch a plain seam and press the seam allowances to one side. Trim the underneath seam allowance to ⅛in (2mm), then turn under the top seam allowance by ¼in (5mm) and pin or baste in place over the trimmed edge. Edge stitch close to the fold, through the seam allowance and the garment. Made like this, the final seam will show two lines of stitching on the right side and a fold and one line of stitching on the reverse.

flax

See linen.

fleece

A fabric made of polyester yarn, sometimes combined with other fibers, which is knitted before the surface is brushed to compact the cloth, trap air and raise the fibers. The surface is then trimmed to create a smooth, even finish. Fleece is a soft fabric that is easy to sew because it does not fray and is available in a wide range of colors and designs. It is very warm for its weight and does not hold water, so is ideal for outer garments.

flexi curve

A strip of metal enclosed in plastic, which can hold its shape if bent into any type of curve. It is used for marking curving lines, either as a guide for stitching or when drawing up templates with curved edges.

floating yarn

Another term for the warp threads in woven fabric. *See also* filling yarn.

FLORENTINE STITCH

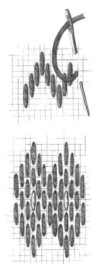

Florentine Stitch

This stitch is used for working zigzag patterns and is generally used to fill a large area, worked in two or more rows of different colors forming a wave pattern. The size of the wave varies, depending on the number of stitches or the number of threads over which the stitches are worked. Also known as Bargello. Both Florentine and Bargello are used to refer to this type of embroidery in general, as well as to the specific stitch. *See also* Byzantine Stitch.

floss

A term for embroidery thread.

flower thread

A single-strand embroidery thread with a fine matte finish, which gives a softer edge than some other embroidery threads but does tend to get dirty quickly. It is available in a good range of colors.

fly

A neatened opening that conceals a zipper or button fastening. Commonly used on pants and topcoats.

fly front zipper/zip

A type of zipper application traditionally used on menswear but which is now often also used in womenswear. One half of the opening is stitched close to the zipper teeth, while the other is a flap that overlaps the opening and typically is stitched in a parallel line to the opening, curving around and under the zipper at the end. See also concealed zipper, lapped zipper, separating zipper.

Fly Stitch

See Y Stitch.

fold line

(1) A visible line across a piece of fabric where it has been folded and the folded edge pressed flat. (2) A marking on pattern pieces, indicating that they should be laid out for cutting with this edge on a lengthwise fold of the fabric. Make sure the marked fold line is exactly on the fabric fold.

Folded Patchwork Blocks

Quilt block designs that are based on folding fabric in various ways. Since there are often several layers of fabric in such blocks, the quilts often need no batting and the backing is built in as the block is assembled. They make ideal lightweight coverlets. Examples are:

Cathedral Window—a large square of fabric is folded corners to middle twice, the diagonal edges are rolled back and stitched in place, four blocks are stitched together into a larger square, then contrasting fabric is inserted under the rolled edges to cover the joins; **Folded Log Cabin**—in which the bars are folded and foundation quilted; **Suffolk Puff/Yo-yo**—in which the edge of a circle of fabric is gathered so that it folds around a piece of batting, the resulting "puffs" of fabric being stitched at the points where the circles touch.

FORBIDDEN KNOT

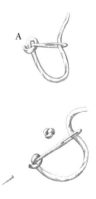

Forbidden Knot
An embroidery stitch that is very similar

to the French Knot, but produces a firmer, more rounded shape. Also known as Blind Knot, Chinese Knot, Peking Knot.

Forbidden Stitch
See Pekinese Stitch.

foulard
A lightweight, twill-weave fabric made from filament yarns such as silk, acetate or polyester, with a small all-over print pattern on a solid background. It is often used for men's ties, handkerchiefs or scarves.

foundation chain
Sometimes also called the starting chain. The initial chain stitches made at the beginning of a crochet project as the base on which the first row or round is worked. To make the chain, start with a slip knot on the hook, bring the yarn over the hook from back to front, and pull through the loop on the hook to make one chain. Continue to make the number of chains specified.

foundation piecing/quilting
Foundation quilts are made by sewing pieces of fabric onto a temporary or permanent foundation. English paper

piecing is one type of foundation quilting; crazy patchwork is another, as the scraps are often stitched to a plain fabric base. Log Cabin can also be made using the foundation method, although it can be made in other ways as well.

Four-legged Knot

This embroidery stitch is worked as an upright cross with a knot at the center. It is often used in crewelwork and may be used as an open filling or just scattered to accent some particular feature.

Four-patch Block

A patchwork block made up of four smaller squares; a basic Four-patch Block has two light and two dark fabric squares. However, the small squares may also be made up of smaller elements. Examples of this include: **Broken Dishes**—each square is made of a light- and dark-colored right-angled triangle and assembed with light and dark alternating around the center; **Pinwheel** or **Windmill**—as Broken Dishes, but put together so that the light and dark alternate around the square; **Double Four-patch**—each square is made up of four smaller light and dark squares.

Blocks can also be put together in different ways, which adds even more complexity to the design.

4-ply

UK term for fingering yarn, a lightweight yarn, which can be wool, cotton, synthetic, or a blend.

Four-sided Stitch

An embroidery stitch worked from left to right, which creates a square outline. It can be used as a border or as a filling.

fractional stitches

A form of Cross Stitch in which only part of the stitch is worked. A complete Cross Stitch has two stitches crossing diagonally at right angles, so a quarter of the stitch is just half of one diagonal stitch, half the stitch is one complete diagonal stitch and three-quarters of the stitch is one complete diagonal with half the other diagonal at right angles. Known respectively as Quarter Stitch, Half Stitch and Three-quarter Stitch.

frame

A piece of equipment to hold a section of a quilt taut while it is being hand quilted. Smaller quilting frames are similar to embroidery hoops, but the hoops are sturdier with a longer bolt on the outer hoop to cope with layers of fabric. A tube frame is made of adjustable tubing with clips on each side to hold the fabric on. Floor-standing frames are also available; *see* frameless quilting.

frameless quilting

Hand quilting without using a frame, usually when working a single block. Frameless quilting is also used to describe working on a floor-standing frame, which holds the quilt taut between two rollers instead of in a frame.

fraying

When the threads begin to separate and pull away at the raw edge of a piece of fabric. Sometimes known as unraveling or raveling.

free-motion machine stitching

Sewing on the machine with the feed dogs lowered or covered and the presser foot removed or replaced with a special attachment, so that the fabric can be moved around at will as you stitch. It is mainly used for machine embroidery and for meander quilting.

freestyle embroidery

A style of embroidery without repeating motifs, in which the design is "painted" in the thread colors.

French curve

French curves are plastic (or wooden) templates with an outline edge composed of several different curves. They are used to draw smooth curves of almost any desired curvature when creating templates or embroidery/quilting designs.

French knitting

Sometimes also called spool knitting. A type of knitting worked on four pegs set around a central hole, creating a circular tube of Stocking Stitch. Insert one end of the yarn in the hole, then wind the yarn clockwise around each of the four pegs, pulling tightly. To start knitting, wrap the yarn around the back of one of the pegs, then lift the wrapped yarn over the top. Keep repeating this all around; the cord will grow from the bottom of the spool.

French knitting doll/dolly

See knitting spool.

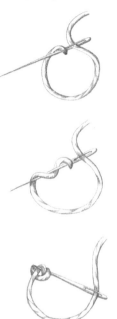

FRENCH KNOT

French Knot

One of the basic embroidery stitches, the French Knot is very versatile. It can be worked on its own as a detail, grouped closely together to form a textured area such as a flower center, worked in a row as a border, or scattered across an area as a filling stitch. *See also* Colonial Knot.

French method

A technique of knitting in which the left needle is held from above by the left hand and the right needle is held by the right hand as if it were a pencil. The yarn is controlled by the forefinger of the right hand.

French seam

A type of seam that adds a professional finish to garments made of lightweight silks or sheers. With wrong sides together, make a seam ½in (1cm) from the edge, then trim the seam allowance to ⅛in (3mm) and press open. Fold the fabric right sides together along the stitching line, press and stitch a seam ¼in (5mm) from the fold. The seam now totally encloses the raw edges. A mock French seam can be made on curved edges. Make a seam in the normal way with a ⅜in (6mm) seam allowance and press open. Fold the edges of the seam towards the stitching line and press, then bring the two folded edges together and whipstitch.

friendship quilt

See album quilt.

frill

A ruffled, gathered or pleated border used to trim clothing. *See also* ruffle.

frogs/frogging

Decorative two-part fasteners that can either be bought or made. Designs can be simple or complex; the simplest design is just four loops in a flower shape, three of which are stitched down to one side of the opening and the fourth left free to slip over the button.

front hip pocket

This type of pocket is made with two different shaped pieces—the pocket, which becomes part of the main section of the garment at the waistline, and the facing, which finishes the opening edge.

front neck-to-waist measurement

This measurement is taken from the shoulder at the base of the neck to the waistline, over the bust/chest.

full fashioning

A term used for a type of shaping in knitting, in which the increases and decreases are worked a few stitches in from the edge and are a feature of the design.

fused hem

A no-sew method of hemming in which the hem is fixed in place with a strip of fusible webbing. Use webbing narrower than the hem and test on a spare piece of fabric first. If the edges show through, pink them first and try not to rest the iron on them when pressing the hem in place. This type of hem is suitable for most types of fabric, but the web will show through very sheer ones. *See also* machine-rolled hem, rolled hem, zigzag hemming.

fusible webbing/interfacing

A fabric with a heat-activated glue on one side, which can be ironed on, usually permanently. Fusible webbing is very fine webbing with glue on both sides; it is used to bond two pieces of fabric together. Fusible interfacing is thicker and has the glue on only one side; it is used to stiffen fabrics.

G

gabardine

A tightly woven, smooth, durable twill-weave fabric of worsted, spun rayon, cotton or various blends. It can have a lustrous or a dull finish, comes in various weights and generally wears extremely well, although it is inclined to shine with wear. Wool gabardine is popular as a fabric for tailored suits and it is also used for coats, raincoats and uniforms.

Garter Stitch

Knitting in Knit Stitch only, which produces a reversible fabric with lines of horizontal ridges on both sides. The same effect can also be produced by purling every row, although this takes longer. Also sometimes known as plain knitting. *See also* Stockinette Stitch.

Garter-stitch selvage

Sometimes also called Seed or Moss Stitch selvage. A knitting technique in which the first and last stitches in each row are knitted, creating ridged edges that are useful as guides when sewing up using Mattress or Flat Stitch.

gathering

To control fullness by running a double line of large stitches through a fabric, fastening the threads at one end and pulling on the other end to reduce the fabric to a smaller length.

Gauge

(1) *knitting/crochet* Refers to tension, the number of stitches/rows within a measured square of the work, usually 4 × 4in (10 x 10cm), in the pattern and using the specified needles/hook. (2) *beading* Measurement that indicates the fineness of beading wire. (3) A tool that is used for measuring the size of needles, crochet hooks, wire or any similar cylindrical material. *See also* tension.

gauze
A thin, sheer, plain-weave fabric made from cotton, wool, silk, rayon, or other manufactured fibers. It is used for curtains, garments, trimmings, and surgical dressings.

georgette
A sheer, lightweight fabric, often made of silk or a manufactured fiber such as polyester, with a crêpe surface. It is used for garments such as dresses and blouses.

German Knot
See Beaded Stitch.

German method
See continental method.

gimp
A narrow flat braid or rounded cord of fabric used for trimming.

gingham
A mediumweight, plain-weave fabric with a plaid or check pattern, usually white plus a color. It is used for dresses, shirts and curtains.

Glove Stitch
See top stitching.

godet
A triangular piece of fabric inserted into the base of a seam at the hem, or into a rectangular cut out with a rounded top at the hem edge of a fabric piece. A godet adds additional fullness at the hem.

goldwork
An embroidery technique that uses metal threads that are either stitched or couched onto the fabric, depending on their weight.

GORDIAN KNOT

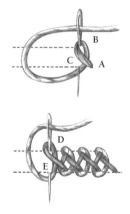

Gordian Knot Stitch
An embroidery stitch worked from right to left as a row of looped knots. It creates a textured border that is also easy to

work around curves, and looks best in heavier threads. It is important to lay the left side of the loop over the right side each time, as shown. Also known as Braid Stitch.

gore
A triangular or tapering piece of fabric, forming a panel in a skirt.

Gore-Tex®
The registered brand name for a range of waterproof breathable fabrics, composed of a thin porous membrane bonded to a base fabric—usually nylon or polyester.

gossamer
A very light, sheer, gauze-like fabric, popular for wedding dresses.

grading
(1) *seams* Trimming raw edges in graduated widths to reduce bulk. The narrowest seam edge should be closest to the body, as a general rule. (2) *beading* Arranging beads of different sizes so that they run in order from large to small or vice versa.

grafting
A knitting technique, also known as Kitchener Stitch or weaving, which is used where a seamless join is required, such as on shoulder seams. Leave both pieces on the needle and lay them out edge to edge with the needles next to one another; with a length of the yarn and a blunt-ended needle, work from right to left. Insert the needle from the back through the first stitch of the lower piece, then through the first stitch of the upper piece, also from the back. Go through the first stitch on the lower piece again, this time from front to back, then bring the needle from back to front through the next stitch on the lower piece. Repeat in this manner along the join, pulling the yarn through as you go but trying to match the tension of the knitted pieces.

grain
In woven fabrics, the lengthwise and crosswise direction of the yarn. When the lengthwise and crosswise grains are at right angles, the fabric is on the "true grain."

Granny Square
A traditional motif in crochet, of which there are countless variations. The simplest is made by working groups of Double (US) or Treble (UK) Stitches

around in a square, sometimes spaced with a chain between. Traditionally the squares were made to use up scraps of yarn, so successive rounds are in different colors.

Greek Cross Filling Stitch

An embroidery stitch used in Hardanger and other drawn-thread work. Wrap two of the fabric threads across the middle, working towards the center of the motif. To work the next bar and the filling, take the thread under the center and up between the next four fabric threads to be worked. Pull the first stitch firmly to tighten, then weave in a figure eight pattern, pulling quite tightly at first, gradually loosening off to make a fan shape. Count the number of stitches so that you can repeat for each motif. Finish wrapping the fabric threads of the second bar; move on to the next section by taking the needle under the next set

---

Crochet Call

When fastening off a project, weave the ends back through with a yarn needle instead of a hook. This makes the ends more secure in the project.

---

of threads to come up on the outer edge and work the corner as before. Work this way in each quadrant until the motif is complete.

grommet

A ring of plastic, metal or rubber that is inserted into a hole in fabric to reinforce it or to protect the edges. May also sometimes be known as an eyelet.

Gros Point Stitch

A bulky embroidery stitch in which a straight stitch is made and then worked over in Tent Stitch from right to left.

Grub Knot

See Bullion Stitch/Knot.

Guilloche Stitch

A composite embroidery stitch, the name of which comes from an architectural term used for a type of ornamental border containing wavy lines. It is used as a decorative border and can be worked in several different colored yarns. The outer edges are two parallel rows of Stem Stitch, with three vertical Satin Stitches worked at even intervals in the center. Weave a thread up and down through alternate groups of Satin Stitches, keeping the loops

GUILLOCHE STITCH

open. Repeat in the opposite way, creating a row of circles, then finish with a French Knot in the center of each circle.

gusset
A small, shaped piece of fabric set into a slash or a seam for added width and ease. In garments it may be found at the underarm, when the sleeves and bodice are cut in one piece, or in the crotch of briefs.

guayabera
A type of men's shirt, probably originating in Cuba, with a straight bottom designed to be worn outside pants. It has two pockets, two above and two below, and two vertical lines of embroidery.

H

habotai

Japanese silk, very lightweight, smooth and soft. It is similar to Chinese silk, although heavier, and is lighter than shantung. It is mainly used for scarves, dresses and blouses. *See also* silk.

haberdashery

UK term for small sewing items, such as thread, needles, pins, zips, buttons, bias binding. Commonly known in the US as notions or sewing notions.

Half Backstitch

This is worked in the same way as Backstitch, but the stitches on the face of the fabric are spaced a little apart rather than butting up to each other. It is used for seams or for decorative effect.

Half Buttonhole

A stitch used in utility quilting, worked as only one "leg" of Buttonhole Stitch set at spaced intervals to create a row of L-shaped stitches.

Half Double Crochet

US term for a crochet stitch that in the UK is called Half Treble Crochet. To make it, wrap the yarn around the hook, insert into the 4th chain from the hook, yarn over and pull through to the front; three loops on the hook. Yarn over and pull through all three loops at once.

Half Stitch

See fractional stitches.

Half Treble Crochet

UK term for a crochet stitch that is between a Double Crochet (UK) and a Treble (UK). The US term for this stitch is Half Double Crochet.

Half-hitch Knot

A knot often used in tatting and macramé. Begin by forming a clockwise loop around the vertical string, with the working end on top. Bring the working end through the loop so that you have an overhand knot. *See also* Double Half-hitch Knot.

ham

Also known as a dressmaker's ham or tailor's ham. This is a tightly stuffed, "ham-leg"-shaped item used at the ironing board to support and provide the appropriate molding for pressing curved areas such as darts and sleeves.

hand/handle

The way a fabric feels when it is touched, such as silky, crisp or soft.

hand sewn

A piece of work that has been stitched by hand with a needle and thread, not with a sewing machine.

hand-stitched buttonhole

A horizontal hand-stitched buttonhole should have Buttonhole Stitch along each side, fanning out in a half circle at the end nearest the edge where the button will rest, with a straight bar tack at the opposite end. A vertical hand-stitched buttonhole should be finished the same at both ends. When working a hand-stitched buttonhole, slash the fabric to the size of the opening and then oversew the edges to stop them from fraying as the buttonhole is stitched.

hank

A length of tapestry wool measuring approximately 60yds (55m) and a length of crewel wool measuring approximately 197yds (180m).

Hardanger

A type of embroidery worked on even-weave fabric and based on blocks of an uneven number of Satin Stitches. After these have been completed, some of the fabric threads are cut and withdrawn, as required. Loose threads are overcast or woven to form bars and various filling stitches worked within the spaces left by withdrawn threads. Also known as Norwegian drawn work. *See also* drawn-thread work.

Hawaiian quilt

A style of quilting that developed on the island of Hawaii, which consists of folding a square of fabric in half twice, then diagonally once and cutting out a shape along the right-angle edges, which when unfolded creates a complex star or snowflake design. This is then appliquéd to a contrasting background fabric, and the whole design is echo quilted by hand. *See also* Scherenschnitte.

heading

(1) *curtainmaking* The fabric tuck above the casing or at the top edge of curtains. (2) *sewing* The narrow edge above a line of gathering forming a frill.

headpin

A pin used in jewelery making, with a flat top like a normal pin—or sometimes a decorative top, but with a blunt tip. It is used at the end of earrings, or for drops on necklaces.

hem

(1) The finished bottom edge of an item. *See also* fused hem, machine-rolled hem, rolled hem, zigzag hemming. (2) To turn over and finish an edge of fabric.

hemline

The line on which a hem is marked and turned to the underside. Skirt and dress hemlines rise and fall with fashion, so may fall anywhere from below the ankle to well above the knee.

Hemming Stitch

A hand-sewing stitch used for all types of hems. Secure the end of the thread at a seam on the wrong side of the item. Take a tiny, inconspicuous stitch in the garment, then take the needle diagonally up through the folded edge of the hem. Continue in this way, spacing the stitches about ¼in (6mm) apart.

hemp

A natural, vegetable-based fiber from the hemp plant (*Cannabis sativa*)—which is the same as the marijuana/cannabis plant used to make narcotics, but cultivated in a different way. Hemp fabric is more water-absorbent than cotton and much stronger.

Herringbone Ladder Filling Stitch

See Interlaced Band.

Quilt Quote

Sashiko patterns have become more sophisticated since the early days and are often abstract designs based on traditional shapes of bamboo, waves and flowers.

HERRINGBONE STITCH

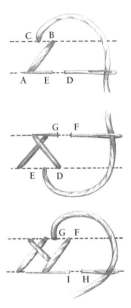

Herringbone Stitch

(1) *embroidery* A basic embroidery stitch, which has many alternative names. It is worked from left to right, in a series of diagonal stitches up and down, crossing slightly at top and bottom. (2) *knitting/sewing* Worked as for embroidery, this stitch is useful to sew hems and facings in place as it has a little more give than plain hemming.

hessian

A coarse cloth woven from jute, a natural vegetable fiber. Jute is inexpensive and easy to spin, but deteriorates quickly if it gets wet. It is often used to make sacking—hessian is also known as sackcloth—or woven into rugs. Hessian is available in a range of bright colors for craft projects.

hip measurement

Take the hip measurement at the widest part, approximately 7–9in (18–23cm) below the waist. When taking the measurement, keep the tape level and parallel to the ground, snug to the body but not too tight.

Holbein Stitch

See Double Running Stitch.

holographic thread

A fine, synthetic thread that sparkles with reflected light and colors. It can be used for both hand and machine embroidery.

HONEYCOMB STITCH

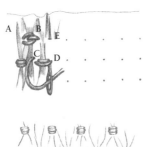

Honeycomb Stitch

An embroidery stitch that is often used in smocking. It consists of groups of three horizontal stitches worked in rows of two at a time, the first three on the upper row, the next three on the lower row, and continuing alternately up and down across the fabric to create a honeycomb look.

Hong Kong finish

Enclosing a seam with bias binding.

hook & eye closure

A type of closure consisting of a small hook on one side and a loop made of fabric or metal on the other. It is used at the upper back of many dresses, above the top of the zipper, and often on lingerie.

hpi

The number of holes (or threads) that a fabric has per inch. The higher the count, the finer the fabric.

I

i-cord

A knitted cord made on double-pointed needles. Cast on four or five stitches; knit one row, then—without turning—push the stitches to the other end of the needle, bring the yarn across the back from left to right and pull tightly. Knit the next row, push the stitches to the end again without turning and repeat until the cord is the right length.

ikat

A style of weaving in which either the warp or the weft threads are tie-dyed before weaving to produce the pattern. If both warp and weft are tie-dyed, it is known as double ikat. The term ikat has come to mean both the process and the fabric that is produced, often a beautiful and subtly patterned silk.

increase

When working crochet, additional stitches are added either in the center or at either end of a row. To add at the center, simply work another stitch in the same place as the one just worked, which will create a peak. To add one stitch at the end of a row, work two stitches into the top of the turning chain of the previous row. To add one stitch at the beginning of a row, place your hook in the small hole to the left of the turning chain before the next stitch. If you need to add more than one stitch at the beginning or end of a row, you will need to work one additional chain for each stitch first.

increase knitwise

To add stitches to a piece of knitting, working in Knit Stitch. The exact method may vary—you can knit into the back of the bar between two stitches, knit into the front and then the back of a stitch before slipping it off the needle, or knit an additional stitch into a stitch one row below.

increase purlwise
To add stitches to a piece of knitting, working in Purl Stitch. This is less common than increasing in Knit Stitch, and the simplest method is to purl into the front and then the back of one stitch before slipping it off the needle.

Indian Filling Stitch
See Antique Stitch.

in-seam buttonhole
A buttonhole that is simply a small opening left in the seam.

inset pocket
This type of pocket is usually found in the side seams of dresses, skirts and pants, and is generally created from separate pieces of fabric either stitched to the seamline on either side or to an extension of the main fabric at the pocket opening.

intarsia
A technique in knitting that creates areas of color, usually worked in Stockinette Stitch. Each color requires a separate ball or bobbin of yarn and the yarns are twisted together where they change over to keep the separate areas as one piece of knitted fabric. With intarsia, the knitted fabric has no yarns stranded across the back, as in Fair Isle.

interfacing
A third layer of fabric between the garment and facings, which gives extra body, shaping and support. *See also* interlining, iron-on.

INTERLACED BAND

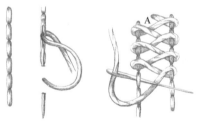

Interlaced Band
A composite embroidery stitch that creates a wide, lacy border. The edge lines are worked as parallel rows of Backstitch, with the stitches of the second row set opposite the stitch breaks of the first. With a contrasting thread, lace right to left through alternate rows as shown, crossing the thread under the needle in the center each time. Also

known as Double Pekinese Stitch, Herringbone Ladder Stitch, Laced Cretan Stitch.

interlining

A fabric placed between the lining and the main fabric. It is used in heavyweight garments such as coats to give added warmth or bulk, in bedspreads to give body, and in curtains to add body and prevent light from showing through.

interlocked canvas

See canvas.

in-the-ditch quilting

A method of understitching also used as a form of simple machine quilting for craft projects. The stitching is done in the seam itself—or very close to a seam allowance—in order to hold it down.

invisible cast on

Also known as provisional cast on. A technique of casting on stitches for a piece of knitting, either for an invisible edge or if the knitting will continue later in the other direction. For the invisible edge type, using a contrast waste yarn of the same weight, cast on half the number of stitches required using the cable method—you will need an even number of stitches, so cast on an extra stitch if required. Knit one row, then purl one row, then using the final yarn for the item work four rows in Stockinette/Stocking Stitch. On the following row, purl one stitch from the left needle, then use the right needle to pick up a loop in the final yarn from the first row and place it on the left needle. Take the yarn to the back and knit this loop. Continue working a purl stitch and picking up a loop and knitting it to the end. When this row is complete, unravel the contrast waste yarn. *See also* cable cast on, chain cast on, long-tail cast on, picot cast on, thumb cast on.

iron-on

(1) *sewing* A chemically treated fabric that can be applied to another fabric using a warm iron. Often used for interfacing or embroidered motifs. (2) *embroidery* A type of embroidery transfer in which the design is on tissue paper and can be transferred to the fabric by ironing on the back with a warm iron.

Italian quilting

See corded quilting.

J

Jacobean Laidwork

An embroidery filling stitch often used in crewelwork and also known as Trellis Couching. Fill the area to be worked with parallel vertical stitches, then work parallel horizontal stitches over the top. In a contrasting thread, and working from right to left, make a diagonal stitch across each crossing point of the base threads. Repeat in the opposite direction to make a small cross stitch at each junction.

jamdani

A type of fine cloth made in Bangladesh and mostly used for saris, but also for scarves and handkerchiefs.

Janina Stitch

See Antique Stitch.

java canvas

See aida.

JACOBEAN LAIDWORK

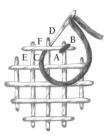  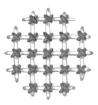

jean jumper
A small piece of plastic to ease sewing seams on denim by holding the presser foot up slightly to allow it to 'jump' the seam as if it was level with the rest of the denim. It works with all thick fabrics.

jerkin
A man's short, close-fitting jacket, without sleeves and buttoning to the neck, usually made of leather.

jewel neckline
A high round neckline to the base of the throat, where a string of pearls would sit.

jersey
A soft, slightly elastic, knit fabric made from cotton, wool or silk. It is mainly used for shirts and dresses.

jiffy lace
See broomstick lace.

jump ring
A small ring with the ends butted together but not fixed, used to join separate sections in jewelery making, and finished pieces to a fastening. To open a jump ring twist the ends away from each other rather than pulling them apart, so that they can be pressed back together without distorting the circular shape.

jumper
(1) A sleeveless, collarless dress designed to be worn over a blouse or sweater. (2) In the UK, a knitted wool pullover or sweater.

jute
A natural vegetable fiber that is woven into a coarse cloth, called hessian. Jute is inexpensive and easy to spin, but deteriorates quickly if it gets wet. It is often used to make sacking—hessian is also known as sackcloth—or woven into rugs. It is available in a wide range of bright colors for craft projects.

K

kantha

A type of quilting that originated in the Bangladesh area of India. It was originally based on securing thin layers of fabric—often old saris—together to form a quilt by using closely spaced stitches in bright colors. The stitching forms motifs, either abstract or geometric designs, or fanciful people, animals, and plants.

kapok

A short, lightweight, cotton-like, vegetable fiber found in the seed pods of the *Bombocaceae* tree. Because of its brittle quality, it is generally not spun—but its buoyancy and moisture resistance make it ideal for use as a filling in cushions, mattresses and life jackets.

keep to pattern

An instruction often found in knitting/crochet patterns indicating that the pattern should be worked as set over the rest of the piece while shaping or other changes are being worked in some areas.

Kensington Outline Stitch

An embroidery stitch used to outline shapes. It is very similar to Stem Stitch, but the needle comes up through the thread of the previous stitch each time, so the line is very straight and neat. Also known as Split Stitch.

kit quilt

Kits containing all the materials needed to make a quilt were very popular from around 1920 to the end of the 1930s. Such quilts are usually quite distinctive and are known collectively as "kit quilts".

kloster block

The basic element of a Hardanger embroidery design, formed by sewing a series of five long Satin Stitches over four threads.

knit fabrics

Fabrics made from only one set of yarns, all running in the same direction. Some knits have their yarn running along the length of the fabric, others have their yarn running across the width of the fabric. Looping the yarn around itself holds knit fabrics together. *See also* rows, wales.

Knit Stitch

The most basic stitch in knitting. To work it, hold the needle with the stitches in the left hand with the yarn at the back, insert the tip of the right needle into the end stitch from left to right, wind the yarn from left to right over the point of the right needle and draw the yarn through the stitch, forming a new stitch on the right needle. Slip the original stitch off the left needle.

KNIT THROUGH BACK LOOP

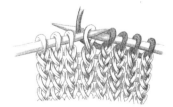

knit through back loop

A knitting technique in which the Knit Stitch is made by inserting the right needle into the back loop of the stitch instead of the front loop. This creates a firmer fabric and is often used in cable patterns to make the design more distinct. *See also* purl through back loop.

knit two together

A knitting technique in which two stitches are knitted at the same time, the simplest method of decreasing. *See also* purl two together.

knitting

Making a knitted fabric with Knit and Purl Stitches—however complex the design, it will have been created with either or both of these two stitches.

knitting needles

The needles used in hand knitting, which are available in a variety of materials including wood, plastic and metal. They come in various lengths to accommodate different numbers of stitches, and in a range of sizes for different yarns or effects. There are three basic types: **plain needles**—a pair of straight sticks with one pointed end and a knob at the other to stop the stitches from slipping off; **circular needles**—two short needle tips joined with a length of nylon or thin metal cord, for knitting in the round or to accommodate wider items; **double-pointed needles**, in sets of four or five with a point at each end, used for knitting in the round or for techniques requiring a change of direction.

knitting ribbon

A type of ribbon designed specifically for knitting, usually available in 1oz (25g) balls.

knitting spool

A circular turned shape around 3in (7.5cm) long with a hole through the center and four small pegs or nails set around the top. It is used for French or spool knitting. A wooden cotton reel or similar with four small nails set in the top can be used as a substitute. Also known as French knitting doll/dolly.

Knitwise

Working a knitted fabric in Knit Stitch.

KNOTTED BUTTONHOLE

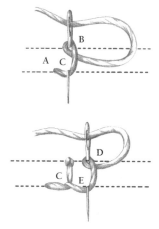

Knotted Buttonhole Stitch

An embroidery stitch that is a slightly more complex version of Buttonhole Stitch, with a knot at the end of each leg. It is very versatile and can be worked in a straight line or in curves.

Knotted Cable Stitch

This embroidery stitch is worked as a

combination of Chain Stitch and Coral Stitch and can be worked in straight lines or in curves. Make one Chain Stitch and then one Coral Stitch; work these two alternately to the end.

Knotted Chain Stitch
See Link Stitch.

Knotted Faggot/Insertion Stitch
Although this embroidery stitch can be worked as a decorative band, it is most often used to join two pieces of fabric. It is worked as normal Faggot/Insertion Stitch, except that the thread is looped around the tip of the needle to form a knot at top and bottom each time.

Knotted Loop Stitch
See Loop Stitch.

Knotted Stitch
See Beaded Stitch.

lace bobbin
A turned length of wood or bone, often very intricate in design, used in bobbin lacemaking with each bobbin holding a single thread.

lace knitting
A type of knitting in which the stitches are cast off and on or knitted together and then remade to make a regular design of holes in imitation of lace.

lace pillow
A firm pillow, traditionally packed with sawdust or straw, used to support the work in bobbin lacemaking.

Laced Cretan Stitch
See Interlaced Band.

Laced Running Stitch
See Cordonnet Stitch.

Ladder
A line of parallel strands of yarn formed in knitting if a stitch is dropped and is allowed to run back some way. This may be a deliberate effect, but otherwise the stitch needs to be worked back up the ladder by pulling one strand of yarn through it to make a new stitch and so on back up to the needle. This may be relatively easy on Stockinette/Stocking Stitch fabric, but it is much harder with other knitted stitches.

Quilt Quote
Wholecloth quilts came from Italy in the 14th century and was very popular in France and England, but was also practiced in other parts of the world.

Ladder Stitch/Hemstitch

An embroidery stitch that is worked downwards and is used as a straight decorative border. To keep the lines straight, draw parallel guidelines before beginning; make a knot on one line, bring the thread across to the other and make a second knot. Continue in this way to make a double line of V-shaped stitches linked by parallel lines of thread. See diagram below. Also known as Open Chain, Step Stitch.

laidwork

See Couching.

laminated

Two or more layers bonded together. Laminated fabric may be constructed of a plastic top and bottom layer, and an intermediate scrim layer, or a waterproof membrane between two layers of fabric.

lap

To extend or fold one piece of fabric or garment section over another.

lapel

A section of a coat, jacket, or blouse that is turned over between the top button and the collar.

lapped band

A narrow band of fabric at a V-shaped neckline that overlaps at the point of the V.

lapped seam

A type of seam that is typically used on non-woven fabrics that do not fray or unravel. Trim away the seam allowance on the upper piece, then lap it over the lower piece with the trimmed edge on the seamline. Edge stitch along

LADDER STITCH

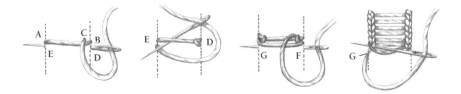

the trimmed edge, then topstitch on the overlap about ¼in (6mm) away from the first line of stitching.

lapped zipper/zip
A zipper inserted in a seam with one side of the seam stitched close to the teeth and the other overlapping. Stitch the seam to the beginning of the zipped opening, then baste the remaining section, press open and finish raw edges. Turn to the inside, extending the right-hand seam allowance, and position the zipper face down centered over the seam and baste in place. Turn the zipper face up, making a fold in the seam allowance close to the teeth, and stitch close to the fold. Turn the garment to the right side and baste the zipper tape to the garment, then topstitch across the end and along the side. *See also* concealed zipper, fly-front zipper, separating zipper.

Lark's Head Knot
A sliding knot used in macramé, jewelry and tatting. Also called Double Stitches in tatting.

latch hook
A tool used for making hooked rugs, with a wooden handle and a metal hook

at one end, and a hinged lever to close the hook.

layering
Trimming the seam allowances in a seam to different widths to reduce bulk.

laying tool
A laying tool, which can also be a large tapestry needle or equivalent, is used to stroke the strands of thread flat near where they emerge from the fabric to help keep the threads untwisted when using several strands.

LAZY DAISY STITCH

Lazy Daisy Stitch
Also known as Detached Chain Stitch, this embroidery stitch consists of individual Chain Stitches worked in a circle to form a little flower.

Leaf Stitch
See Fir Stitch.

leather

A strong, hardwearing material, the hide, pelt or skin of an animal, usually a cow, which has been tanned. It is most commonly available in three different types: full-grain leather—the finest raw material, clean hides with a natural grain, which is strong, durable, comfortable and wears well over time; corrected or top-grain—leather made from inferior material, fuzzy on one side and smooth on the other where the natural grain has been sanded off and replaced with a stamped artificial grain; suede—the interior split of the hide, which is fuzzy on both sides, less durable than top-grain and cheaper because many pieces of suede can be split from a single thickness of hide.

leather end finding

A metal fastening used in jewelry making, with a flap that can be bent over the end of a leather thong and tightened with pliers to grip.

left front

Usually the left section of the front of a garment, when worn.

LEFT TWIST

left twist

(1) *yarn See* twist. (2) *knitting* Knitted cables and twisted stitches can twist to the left (clockwise) or to the right (counterclockwise). *See also* cable4front.

lengthwise fold

A fold down the length of a piece of fabric. Fabric on a bolt is generally folded lengthwise, right sides together.

lightbox

A box with a frosted acrylic (or glass) sheet as a top, which is lit from inside. It is used to transfer designs; the design motif is laid on the box with the fabric on top. As long as the fabric is not too opaque the light shines through both, so the design lines can be traced over onto the top fabric. A backlit window makes an acceptable substitute for small projects.

linen

Linen is a cellulose fiber obtained from the flax plant. Its natural color is off-white or tan and, due to its wax content, it has a natural luster. It is the strongest of the vegetable fibers and is highly absorbent, allowing moisture to evaporate quickly. It washes well but is prone to creasing. Linen is used for garments, accessories, curtains, upholstery, tablecloths and towels.

lining

A fabric that covers the underside of another fabric that has been made up into an item, to conceal the seam construction—as in jacket lining, curtain lining. Garment linings are usually of a slippery fabric and make an item easier to put on and remove. If the garment is washable, the lining should be too.

LINK STITCH

Link Stitch

Also known as Knotted Chain Stitch, this is an embroidery stitch that is most often used to create a straight decorative line. Each individual Chain Stitch is worked as a knot, linked with a simple Straight Stitch.

Lock Stitch

A stitch used in tatting to create a break in the chain tension, which forces the chain to turn in on itself at an angle. It is used when starting with a chain, and when moving from a central ring into a chain or split ring. Lock Stitch is very simple: make the first half of the double stitch, but don't allow it to flip; then make the second half of the double stitch as usual.

Log Cabin Block

A pieced block in quilting, one of the first blocks that many quilters learn, which has many variations. It is based on a central shape, usually a square, surrounded by strips of fabric in concentric rows. The design can look very different depending on how the colored strips are laid and how the blocks are set. Some popular designs include: **Barn Raising**—in which the basic block is half light and half dark and set to create concentric, diamond-shaped bands; **Straight Furrow**—in which the same block is set to create diagonal stripes; **Courthouse Steps**—with light and dark strips set opposite one another in the block; **Sunshine & Shadow**—in which the blocks are set so that the bands of color go from light to dark and back again.

Long and Short Satin Stitch
A simple variation on Satin Stitch, used to fill in areas or motifs. The first row is worked as alternate long and short stitches, then the following rows are long stitches, each of which interlocks with the previous row. A final row of long and short stitches makes a neat, straight edge. By using different shades of the same color on each row, subtle shaded effects can be achieved.

Long-armed/legged Cross Stitch
Cross Stitch used in embroidery and worked so that the diagonal base stitch is twice as long as the upper stitch that crosses it. The next base stitch begins immediately below the point at which the top of the upper stitch enters the fabric and crosses over the upper stitch towards the bottom, so creating an upper and lower line of staggered crossed stitches. Also known as Plaited Slav Stitch, Twist Stitch.

Long-armed Feather Stitch
See Cretan Stitch.

long-tail cast on
A method of casting on stitches to begin a piece of knitting, using one needle, also known as the continental method or double cast on. Place a slip knot on a needle, leaving a long tail of yarn, and hold the needle in the right hand. Wrap the end of the yarn around your left thumb from front to back, place the other end of the yarn over the left forefinger and hold both threads in your palm. Slip the tip of the needle up through the loop on the thumb and over the yarn on the forefinger, drawing it through the loop on the thumb. Transfer the loop from thumb to needle and pull to tighten. Repeat until the correct number of stitches is on the needle. *See also* cable cast on, chain cast on, invisible cast on, picot cast on.

loop method
A method of securing a thread before beginning Cross Stitch, used when stitching with an even number of strands. Cut your thread twice as long

as you need it for stitching, fold it in half and thread the needle, putting the loop at the long end. Bring the needle up through the fabric in the right place to start stitching, leaving about 2in (5cm) of thread on the wrong side. Push the needle back down to form the first half of the Cross Stitch, slipping it through the loop on the back, then pull the thread tight. *See also* waste knot.

LOOP STITCH

Loop Stitch

(1) *embroidery* A stitch that creates a decorative band, worked as a row of vertical straight stitches joined across the center with a knot. Also known as Centipede Stitch, Knotted Loop Stitch. (2) *crochet* A crochet stitch that forms a loop of yarn on the front of the fabric, which may be left or cut through to create a "fur" effect—hence it is also called Fur Stitch. To work it, insert the hook into the stitch below as usual and, using the finger of the free hand, pull up the yarn to form a loop of the required length. Pick up both strands of the loop and draw them through, wrap the free yarn over the hook, and draw the yarn through all three loops.

Lurex®

The registered brand name for a range of high-quality metallic yarn and for the fabrics woven from such yarns.

Lycra®

The registered brand name for elastane or spandex fabric.

M

machine stitched
Sewn on a sewing machine, either by hand or commercially.

machine-rolled hem
A narrow hem that is ideal for sheers, lightweight silk, synthetic fabrics and for hemming frills and ruffles, but you will need a hem allowance of at least ½in (12mm). Mark the hemline ⅛in (3mm) longer than required, fold along this line and machine stitch close to the fold. Do not press the hem before stitching, as if the hemline is not on the straight grain, it will distort the fabric. Using embroidery scissors, carefully trim the hem allowance away above the stitching, then fold the hem allowance up along the stitching line, rolling the stitching line slightly to the inside as you go. Press, machine stitch close to the inner fold and press again. If you are making this hem on translucent fabric, make the first row of stitching in basting/tacking stitches, then you can remove them when the hem is complete. *See also* fused hem, rolled hem, zigzag hemming.

macramé
A craft in which cord or string is knotted in patterns to make decorative articles. Macramé dates back to the mid-19th century and the name is French, but is possibly based on an Arabic word for a bedspread.

madras
A lightweight, plain-weave cotton fabric with a striped, plaid, or checked pattern, usually imported from India. A true madras will bleed when washed. This type of fabric is used for shirts and dresses.

make one
Adding an extra stitch to the needle

while knitting. Patterns often do not specify which method to use and the instruction is abbreviated as m1. *See* increase knitwise, increase purlwise.

MALTESE CROSS STITCH

Maltese Cross Stitch

A large, laced embroidery stitch that can be scattered across an area as a stand-alone motif or worked in a row to make a wide, decorative border. It is worked as a lattice of crossing straight stitches, which are then laced with a contrasting thread. Varying the spacing of the initial lattice gives very different effects.

mandarin collar

Also known as standing collar. A narrow collar that stands up straight from the neckline. The neck edge of the collar is very straight, compared to the curve of the neckline. *See also* flat collar, Peter Pan collar, reverse rolled collar, shawl collar.

masking tape

Low-tack tape that can be used to temporarily fix pieces together, but which can be torn or removed easily without damaging surfaces when no longer required.

matelassé

A medium- to heavyweight luxury fabric made in a double-cloth construction to create a blistered or quilted surface. It is often used for upholstery and evening dresses.

Mattress Stitch

A method of joining two knitted pieces of fabric together with an invisible seam that creates a strong, neat join. The two edges to be joined are butted up to each other, right sides facing up, and the joining stitches are worked either a whole or a half stitch in from the edge in a weaving technique that duplicates the look of a knitted stitch. Also known as Ladder Stitch, Running Stitch.

Meander Stitch
A machine-stitched version of stippling, used in quilting. The machine needs to be set to free-motion working with the embroidery foot in place, and the stitching is worked as a line that wanders at random over the area to be quilted, twisting and turning in tight curves.

medallion quilt
A quilt designed with a central medallion, which can be round, star-shaped or a square on point, surrounded by a series of borders. The medallion can be large, taking up most of the area, or smaller. Medallions are one of the oldest types of quilt design.

Medici wool
A fine French wool, originally produced for the Aubusson carpets. It is finer than crewel wool and is easily divisible. It gives a very smooth finish when sewn.

melton
A heavyweight, dense, compacted and tightly woven wool or wool-blend fabric used mainly for coats. It is either twill- or satin-weave but is felted, giving a smooth surface with a fine nap. It wears well and is very wind resistant, so it is used for heavy outer garments and coats.

mend
To repair or fix a hole, tear, split or other problem with a garment. This can be done by using sew-on or iron-on patches, or stitching by machine or hand. *See also* darn.

Mennonite Tack
A stitch used in utility quilting, a horizontal cross with a long arm crossed near one end by a short arm.

mercerized
A finish for cotton that adds strength and luster and makes the fibers more receptive to dyes.

merino
Wool yarn from the merino sheep, which is the most numerous sheep in the world. Good-quality merino wool is widely regarded as being the finest and softest of the wool yarns.

metal or metallic thread/yarn
A thread or yarn made of pure metal, but also sometimes used for synthetic threads with the appearance of metal.

metallic-effect thread/yarn
A synthetic thread or yarn with the appearance of metal.

metallized thread/yarn
A thread or yarn made with a thin layer of real metal, over a nylon or polyester core for strength and flexibility.

meterage/metreage
The length of yarn or fabric expressed in meters. Balls of yarn give the meterage on the ball band, spools of thread often have it marked on top of the spool. Pattern envelopes give the meterage of fabric required to make the garment in various widths of fabric, and often alternative amounts for fabric with and without a nap.

Methodist Knot
A stitch used in utility quilting, with a long stitch followed by a short stitch, spaced in a row, giving an interesting "dash-dot" effect.

miss
UK term for going past a stitch or a row in knitting or crochet without working it. US term is skip.

miter/mitre
A way of controlling excess fullness when two sections of hem meet at a square corner. With narrow hems a miter can be formed by folding the fabric diagonally across the point of the hemline, then folding the two sides in on the hemlines and catching the two sides of the hem along the diagonal line. With wider hems, fold the fabric diagonally across the point as before, then open out and fold the entire piece right sides together diagonally across the point at right angles to the first fold, so that the hemlines meet. Stitch along the first fold line, then trim off the triangular point close to the seam; press open, then turn the hems back through to the inside and press again.

mock cuff
A false cuff, made by making a tuck in the fabric of the sleeve, which gives the look of a cuff but with a minimum amount of extra fabric. To create it, you will need an extra amount of ½in

(12mm) on the length of a straight sleeve. Fold the bottom of the sleeve to the inside along the hemline, then fold under again by the same amount. Stitch ¼in (6mm) from the second fold, which will create a tuck and hide the raw edge. Fold the doubled fabric back out to the right side; the bottom section of the sleeve will be a double thickness of fabric with a line of stitching at the top below a small stand-up tuck.

mohair

A natural fiber from the Angora goat, sometimes woven with a cotton warp when made into fabric. Mohair yarn is also often hand knitted. It is used for sweaters, coats, suits and scarves. Imitation mohair is made from wool or a wool blend. *See also* angora.

moiré

A fabric with a rippled or watered effect, traditionally silk but now often synthetic. The effect is most pronounced on a plain-colored fabric. Moiré fabrics are used for curtains and other soft furnishings that do not need to be laundered regularly.

mola

A type of quilt from islands in the Atlantic off Panama, based on the reverse appliqué technique and usually featuring birds, animals and village life. The predominant colors are red, black and orange, but other colors are also used in small amounts. All areas are appliquéd on a mola, with the design expanded to fill the piece and abstract designs used to fill any spaces.

MOCK CUFF

mono canvas
See canvas.

monofilament nylon
A transparent thread used in beading, often for intricate weaving projects and necklaces where the beads hang with no apparent means of support. It is not very strong, so should not be used for general threading.

monogram
A letter—usually an initial—embroidered or appliquéd on a garment or other item.

Montenegrin Cross Stitch
A composite embroidery stitch that is very similar to Long-armed/legged Cross Stitch, but also incorporates a vertical Straight Stitch. It is worked from left to right and creates the same effect on both sides of the fabric.

Mosaic Block
A quilting block designed around piecing together small pieces of fabric in regular, repetitive patterns. The component pieces are geometric shapes—squares, triangles, hexagons—set in a variety of patterns and sometimes as small as ⅜in (9mm). A

popular mosaic pattern is made up of small diamonds assembled into the shape of a large star or sunburst the size of the quilt top, creating a dramatic and graphic effect. Some other well-known mosaic designs are: **Grandmother's Flower Garden**—in which the blocks are hexagonal and are arranged to create secondary hexagonal patterns across the quilt; and **1000 Pyramids** in which triangles are sewn alternately up and down next to one another in rows.

MOSAIC STITCH

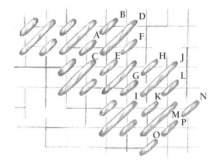

Mosaic Stitch
An embroidery stitch in which long and short diagonal stitches are worked alternately, with the long stitches interlocking with the short on the following row.

Moss Stitch

(1) *knitting* The UK term for Seed Stitch, a knitted stitch pattern created by working an uneven number of stitches in alternate Knit and Purl Stitches, so that in each of the following rows, the Knit Stitch sits on top of the Purl Stitch and vice versa. It creates a hard-wearing and attractive textured fabric. (2) *embroidery See* Cross and Twist Stitch.

Moss Stitch selvage

See Garter Stitch selvage. Also known in the US as Seed Stitch selvage.

motif

(1) *crochet* A shape made using rounds of crochet, which can be square, round or any geometric shape, and which can either stand alone or be joined with others into a larger piece of fabric. (2) *fabric* A repeating element of a printed design. (3) *appliqué* A shaped piece of fabric to be appliquéd to a background.

Mountmellick

A form of white work that has no open or drawn spaces. The stitches lie as much as possible on the surface of the material, with as little thread as possible underneath. It is a coarse form of embroidery, producing the maximum effect for the minimum effort.

muslin

(1) *US* In the US, a fabric made from unbleached—and often not fully processed—cotton. It is less coarse and thick than canvas or denim, but it is cheap and is often used to make couture garments to test the fit before they are made up in the final fabric. *See also* calico. (2) *UK* A smooth, delicately woven cotton fabric, used for dresses and curtains.

N

nainsook
A lightweight, plain-weave cotton fabric, usually with a luster. It is most commonly used for infants' wear, blouses and lingerie.

nap
A soft fabric surface, made by the short fibers being brushed in one direction. Depending on which way the light falls on the fabric, it looks lighter or darker—so the nap should run in the same direction on each part of a garment when it is worn. Patterns may give special cutting layouts to allow for this, and may specify extra fabric.

natural fibers/fibres
Fibers made from the products of plants or animals—for example, silk from the cocoon of the silkworm, wool from the fleece of a sheep, cotton from the cotton plant.

neaten
To finish off by pulling loose threads to the wrong side and tying or stitching them in before cutting off. Seam edges can be neatened and prevented from fraying by binding, pinking, or zigzag stitching.

neckband
A narrow strip of fabric around the neckline of a garment to finish it. In dressmaking, it is made as a separate piece and stitched on; in knitting and crochet, it can be made either as part of the main pieces, or afterwards by picking up stitches around the neckline and working an additional new strip.

needle
Needles are used for stitching fabrics together and there is a wide range of different types for both machine and hand sewing. Sewing-machine needles

include: **ballpoint**—used for knits; **sharps**—used for regular fabrics; **wing**—with wide, wing-shaped, flared sides, used to create holes in tightly woven fabrics as when creating entredeux, and available as single or doubles. Hand-sewing needles include: **betweens**—short, sharp needles, used for hand quilting; **crewel**—sharp pointed and with a long, narrow eye; **darner**—extra-long general-purpose needle; **embroidery**—medium sharp with an oval eye, suitable for crewel work, embroidery and smocking; **sharps**—long, sharp needles suitable for general sewing; **tapestry**—medium, blunt needle with an oval eye, suitable for almost all counted-thread work and ranging in size from 14 (heaviest) to 26 (finest); **universal**—with a slightly rounded tip for woven or knit fabrics; **upholstery**—curved needle to stitch from one side only.

needleboard

A board covered in short, dense needles, which is used when pressing pile fabrics to prevent the pile becoming crushed.

needle felting

A technique for producing three-dimensional objects in felt, by shaping them roughly and at a much larger scale in wool fleece, then stabbing the shape with a special needle to compress the fibers. The needle is very sharp and has barbs at intervals to catch the wool fibers. This type of felting does not require hot soapy water. *See also* felt.

needle gauge

A small piece of metal or plastic with a series of numbered holes, used to establish the size of unmarked knitting needles. A similar piece of equipment is available for crochet hooks.

needle grabber

A small rubber disk that is used to grip the needle and pull it through several layers of fabric, or when working with heavy fabrics.

needle lace

First developed in the 17th century, needle lace is created by using a needle to stitch hundreds of tiny stitches together to make a fine, open fabric; traditionally, only a needle, thread and scissors are used. The main, heavier guiding threads are sewn onto a stiff background, such as thick paper, with removable stitches and the work is then built up using a variety of stitches. When the entire area is covered with the stitching, the removable stitches are released and the lace comes away from the paper. A variety of different styles developed, each with its own name, such as Alençon, Hollie Point, Point de France, Point de Gaze/Gauze, Point de Venise, and Punto in Aria or Reticella.

needle threader

A piece of equipment to make threading small needles much easier. There are various designs, but the most common is a shaped piece of metal with a very thin wire loop at the tip, which fits through the needle eye, opens out to take the thread and is pulled back through taking the thread with it.

needlepoint

A type of embroidery on even-weave canvas, most often worked in wool yarn. It is also known as canvas work or tapestry—although true tapestry is woven on a loom, not stitched.

needle-turned appliqué

An appliqué technique in which the very edge of the motif to be applied is turned under with the tip of the needle just before it is stitched in place.

NEEDLEWEAVING STITCH

Needleweaving Stitch

A stitch used in drawn-fabric embroidery. First, withdraw the number of threads required; then work blocks of weaving to fill the space, making an even number of stitches in each block.

net/netting

A fine-meshed fabric, usually based on a square or a hexagonal grid.

DOUBLE NINE-PATCH BLOCK

Nine-patch Block

One of the most versatile quilting blocks, which in its simplest form is nine squares arranged three by three in a chequerboard pattern. However, the squares can be pieces from smaller elements and the blocks set to create a series of complex patterns. These include: **Double Nine-patch**—with alternate squares of the Nine-patch made up of an even smaller Nine-patch block; **Single Irish Chain**—formed by setting Nine-patch blocks with large plain squares; and **Shoofly**—in which the corners are pieced triangles in contrasting fabrics, with the center square matching the inner triangle and the four surrounding squares matching the outer triangle.

ninon

A lightweight, plain-weave fabric, made either from silk or manufactured fibers, with an open, mesh-like appearance. Since the fabric is made with high-twist filament yarns, it has a crisp hand. End uses include eveningwear and curtains.

noil

A type of silk, sometimes incorrectly called raw silk, with a nubby feel and a low sheen. The nubby texture comes from the yarn, which is woven with very short fibers, so it has occasional slubs and loose ends. Noil resembles cotton in surface texture, and has a gentle drape. It is durable, travels well and resists wrinkles, so it is good for most types of garments.

non-woven fabric

Engineered fabric made by bonding or entangling fibers or filaments together, rather than by using weaving or knitting. The fabric is made directly from separate fibers or from molten plastic or plastic film—the fibers do not have to be made into yarn. Non-woven fabrics have no grain and may have a limited life or be very durable—examples include batting/wadding, interlining and felt.

Norwegian drawn work

See Hardanger.

notches

V-shaped marks on the cutting line of a pattern, indicating matching points on a seam. Notches on separate pattern pieces are matched up when they are seamed together. Notches should be marked when cutting out, usually by cutting around them so that they protrude. Some people cut them into the seam allowance instead—but this is not a good idea, particularly if the fabric is liable to fray.

notions
Small sewing items, such as thread, needles, pins, zippers, buttons, and bias binding. *See* haberdashery.

nuno felt
A felting technique in which the wool fibers are felted onto a translucent fabric base. The fabric provides stability for the piece, so less wool is used and the item can be light and translucent—unlike normal felt, which is quite thick and opaque.

nylon
Developed in 1938, nylon was the first completely synthetic fiber. It is very strong and resistant to both abrasion and to many chemicals. It is elastic, flexible, easy to wash, returns well to its original shape and is fast drying. It is also non-absorbent, resistant to water, perspiration and some dyes, as well as to moths and other insects.

oilcloth

A vinyl fabric supported on a mesh of woven cotton, usually with a vibrant, colorful design. It is generally used where a wipe-clean surface is desirable, such as for chair seats, tablecloths, beach bags, or children's bibs.

Old English Knot Stitch

See Smyrna Stitch.

on point

A quilting term indicating a square block set so that it rests on one corner, rather than on one of the straight edges.

one-way designs

Designs based on motifs with a distinct top and bottom, so they run in only one direction and look different if the fabric is turned upside down. When laying out pattern pieces on one-way fabric, use the layout for napped fabric to be sure that the design will run the same way visually on the finished garment.

Open Chain

See Ladder Stitch.

Open Cretan Stitch

A version of basic Cretan Stitch, in which the stitches are spaced apart. It is worked from right to left and is good for both straight lines and for curves.

Open Fishbone Stitch

An embroidery stitch used for filling motifs. It is based on Straight Stitch worked diagonally and alternately, with the ends of the stitches just interlocking. It is the same as Fishbone Stitch, except that the stitches are spaced slightly apart.

Open Loop Stitch

See Y Stitch.

open-ended zipper/zip
See separating zipper.

openweave
A fabric that is loosely woven, so that there are gaps between the threads. An extreme example is netting, but linen and aida are also openweaves.

organdy
A fine, translucent cotton fabric that is usually stiffened and is used for dresses and blouses.

organza
A transparent, lightweight fabric of silk or a synthetic yarn, sometimes with a silvery sheen. It is creases quite easily, but is easy to iron. It is used for evening-wear and to line items that need to be stiffened without adding weight.

Oriental Stitch
See Antique Stitch.

ottoman
A tightly woven, plain-weave, ribbed fabric with a slight luster. The ribbed effect is created by weaving a finer silk or man-made warp yarn with a heavier weft yarn, usually of cotton or wool. The heavier weft yarn is completely covered by the warp yarn, creating the ribbed effect. It is used for coats, suits, dresses, upholstery, and draperies.

OVERCAST BARS

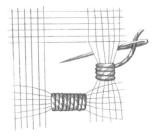

Overcast Bars
A stitch used in Hardanger and drawn-thread embroidery. Withdraw the number of threads required, then separate the loose threads into bars by overcasting to cover them completely. Also known as Wrapped/Whipped Bar Stitch. *See also* Woven Bars.

overcasting
A row of diagonal hand stitching done over raw edges, particularly of a seam, to prevent them from fraying or ravelling. This can also be done by machine, and some sewing machines have a special stitch setting. Also known as oversewing, or overstitching.

Overhand Knot
A simple knot used in many needle-crafts. To work it, hold the yarn or string out parallel to the ground and cross it over to form a loop. Wrap the right-hand end through the loop, and pull.

overlap/overwrap
The part of a garment or other item that extends over another.

overlock
An overcast stitch to prevent fraying or ravelling of raw fabric edges. Some sewing machines do overlock stitching. *See also* serger.

oversewing
See overcasting.

Oxford
A fine, soft, heavy, woven cotton, sometimes blended with man-made fibers, woven in a basketweave and used mainly for shirts.

P

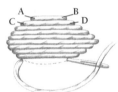

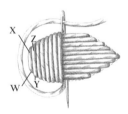

Padded Satin Stitch

An embroidery stitch that is simply basic Satin Stitch worked horizontally, then worked over the top vertically to create a raised motif. It can also be used to create a raised band by working the first stitches from side to side the width of the band, then working the second stitches diagonally over the top. Also known as Raised Satin Stitch.

paisley

A distinctive repeating pattern of teardrop shapes with a curved point, usually printed but sometimes embroidered. It is named after the town of Paisley in Scotland, where it was first made.

Palestrina Stitch

See Smyrna Stitch.

pass next stitch over

A technique in knitting in which the next stitch is passed over, or slipped from one needle to the other, without being worked. The stitch will need to be passed either knitwise or purlwise, as this affects how it sits on the needle. *See also* slip one knitwise, slip one purlwise.

pass slipped stitch over

A knitting technique used to decrease by one stitch. Slip the stitch from left needle to right without working it, then, work the next stitch and lift the slipped stitch over it and off the needle.

patch pocket

A pocket made of a separate piece of fabric applied to the front surface of a garment like an open top patch. Patch pockets can be any size or shape, and may be lined or unlined.

patchwork

Joining together smaller pieces of fabric to make a larger piece. Patchwork techniques are often used in quilting, but patchwork fabric can also be used for other things and does not have to be quilted—although it may require backing to hide all the construction seams. Also known as piecing.

pattern repeat

Most patterns are not just one motif but are made up of one or more components that repeat along the length and/or width. The length of a pattern repeat is determined by measuring from a set point on a motif to the matching point on the next. In a half-drop repeat, alternate rows of motifs are repeated half a repeat down, so creating secondary diagonals. In a full-drop repeat, the rows are all repeated with the motifs in line both down and across. *See also* one-way designs.

pattern weights

Weights used to hold down paper patterns instead of pinning the pieces to the fabric.

peaks

A term used in appliqué to denote a sharp, upward point. *See also* valleys.

Pearl Stitch

An embroidery stitch that is mainly used for outlining and can be worked in a straight line or in a curve. It is basically a Straight Stitch with a knot at the end, creating a beaded line. The beads can be spaced at any distance by varying the length of the Straight Stitch.

peau de soie

A smooth, finely ribbed, medium-to-heavy satin fabric made of silk, polyester or rayon with a good drape and a dull luster. The name comes from the French and literally means "skin of silk." It is mainly used for evening gowns and wedding dresses.

PEKINESE STITCH

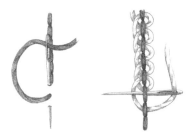

Pekinese Stitch

A composite embroidery stitch mainly used as a border, which can be worked in a straight line or round a curve. It is made up of a line of Backstitch, which is then whipped with a contrasting thread in a circular motion. Also known as Blind Stitch, Chinese Stitch, Forbidden Stitch.

Peking Knot

See Forbidden Knot.

Pendant Chain Stitch

See Petal Stitch.

penelope canvas

An embroidery canvas woven with double threads, creating both wide and narrow spaces, so the effect of two meshes can be created on one canvas by using the large holes for background and

the small holes for detail areas. The mesh count is listed in two number mesh sizes – for example, 10/20, 14/28, or 18/36. It is also known as duo canvas or double-thread canvas.

percale

A mediumweight, plain-weave, low-to-medium count (180–250 threads per square inch) cotton-like fabric. It is used for bedsheets, blouses and dresses.

Persian Stitch

See Cretan Stitch.

Persian wool/yarn

A stranded yarn, usually of wool, that is used for embroidery work. It can be divided into single strands and used for finer work.

Petal Stitch

A composite embroidery stitch used for outlining, which works well both as a straight and a curved line. It consists of a line of Stem Stitches, with a single Chain Stitch worked off each one so that it hangs down beneath the line. Also known as Pendant Chain Stitch.

Peter Pan collar

A small collar with rounded points, often

used on children's clothes. It may be flat or rolled. *See also* flat collar, mandarin collar, revers rolled collar, shawl collar.

petit point
This refers to both the needlecraft and the canvas. The canvas is very fine, with 17 or more holes per inch. The needlecraft uses Tent Stitch in wool or silk on petit point canvas to achieve fine detail and wonderful shading. *See also* Tent Stitch.

PICKING UP A DROPPED STITCH

picking up stitches
A technique in knitting, which is most often used when a border must be added to an edge, worked at right angles to the main piece. To pick up stitches evenly, divide the edge into equal sections first and calculate how many stitches need to be picked up in each section. Stitches can be picked up using a needle, or a crochet hook on tightly knitted pieces. Insert the needle or hook into the stitch just below the edge, wrap the yarn around and pull through to form a new stitch. Continue as required. This term may also be used to denote picking up a dropped stitch, as illustrated.

Picot
(1) *tatting* A space of passive thread in a loop between two double stitches, used for joining or for decoration. (2) *knitting/crochet* A row of decorative points made along an edge or border. *See also* picot cast on and bind/cast off.

picot cast on
A technique of casting on to begin a piece of knitting that gives a pretty edge with a row of little points, which is particularly suitable for collars and cuffs. It is worked by casting on and binding/casting off stitches in order—for instance: cast on four stitches using the cable method, bind/cast off two stitches, slip the stitch left on the right needle back onto the left; repeat this sequence until you have the correct number of stitches. *See also* cable cast on, chain cast on, invisible cast on, long-tail cast on, thumb cast on.

picot cast/bind off

A technique of finishing a knitted piece that gives a pretty edge with a row of little points, which is particularly suitable for collars and cuffs. It is worked by casting/binding off and casting on stitches in order—for instance: cast/bind off four stitches, slip the stitch left on the right needle back onto the left, cast on two stitches; repeat this sequence until you have one stitch left, then fasten off.

piecing

Joining together smaller pieces of fabric to make a larger piece, also known as patchwork. Many quilt blocks are pieced. *See also* curved blocks, Four-patch Block, Nine-patch Block, Log Cabin, Mosaic Block, stitch-and-flip.

pile

Raised threads or loops on the surface of a fabric. Pile may also have a nap.

pilling

When yarns are knitted or crocheted into a fabric, wear or laundering can cause the loose surface fibers to bunch up into little balls of fluff stuck to the surface of the fabric. This is known as pilling. These balls can be shaved off or carefully picked off to improve the look of the item.

pin cushion

A small, padded cushion used to hold pins when not in use. Some pin cushions have an band of elastic attached, so that they can be worn on the wrist as you work for quick access to the pins.

pin tuck

A narrow, stitched tuck in fabric. Several are often made in close parallel rows to give a decorative look to a garment. Some blouses are made with pin tucking on the bodice for a tailored look.

pinked seam

See stitch and pink.

pinking shears

A special pair of scissors with zigzag-edged blades instead of straight ones,

---

Stitch Wit

Clip the selvages when working with long lengths of fabric, such as in curtains or drapes. Selvedges are tightly woven and should be clipped to be sure the fabric lies flat and naturally for cutting.

---

which cut a zigzag—or pinked – line instead of a straight one. They are used to finish seam edges when the fabric does not fray.

PIPING

piping
A cord covered with fabric, often used as a decorative edging on garments or projects. It is usually inserted into a seam and can match or contrast with the main fabric.

piqué
A stiff fabric with a strong rib or raised pattern, usually made of cotton but sometimes of rayon or silk. It is used to make garments.

pivot
To lift the presser foot and turn the fabric on the machine needle without lifting the needle from the fabric. Used when stitching square corners.

place marker
Also known as stitch markers. A small split ring, usually made in brightly colored plastic, used in knitting/crochet to mark the start of increasing/decreasing or the beginning of new rounds/rows when working circular pieces.

placket
A finished opening, often leading to a pocket or over a concealed zipper or press fasteners, or the flap of fabric behind such an opening.

placket band
An overlapping band at an opening, typically at the base of a neck opening, which may be just decorative or a functional opening with fastenings. For women, it should cross right over left; for men, left over right.

plaid
See tartan.

Plaited Braid Stitch
A complex, looped embroidery stitch, which creates a wide border. It is worked downwards and the effect is better in heavier thread. To keep the loops even, draw guidelines before starting. It may also be easier to pin the loops in place

temporarily as you work.

Plaited Slav Stitch
See Long-armed/legged Cross Stitch.

plastic canvas
See canvas.

BOX PLEAT AND KNIFE PLEATS

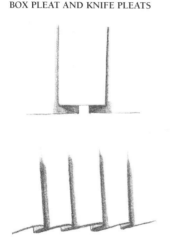

pleat
Even folds in fabric to add fullness, usually at the hem and often partly stitched down just below the waist. The different types are: **accordion** – fine narrow pleats usually made by machine; **box** – two knife pleats that turn away

from each other; **Dior** or **kick** – a short pleat at the hemline of a skirt with a layer of fabric under the opening; **inverted** – two knife pleats that turn towards each other; **knife**—a series of pleats in the same width and in the same direction; **release** – a partly stitched pleat at the top or bottom of a lining to give ease of movement; **sunray** – a pleat that is wider at the bottom than at the top, usually machine made. *See also* curtain pleats.

pleat tape
A stiff tape with woven pockets and draw cords, used to make curtain headings. It is available in different materials and different widths.

pliers
Tools used in jewelry and other types of work using fine wire. They come in various shapes, but the most useful for this type of work are: **flat-nosed**, with flat jaws for creating sharp angles and straight lines, and **round-nosed**, with cone-shaped, round jaws to create curves and circular wire eyes.

plissé
A lightweight, plain-weave fabric made from cotton, rayon or acetate, and

characterized by a puckered, striped effect, usually in the warp direction. The crinkled effect is created through the application of a caustic soda solution, which shrinks the fabric in the areas where it is applied. Plissé is similar in appearance to seersucker and is used for things such as dresses, shirting, pajamas, and bedspreads.

ply
The individual strands of fiber that are spun into yarn. Many yarns are described by the number of plies they are made up of, for instance 4-ply (fingering). *See also* twist.

point protector
A small piece of flexible plastic or rubber with two holes for the needles to slip into, used to prevent knitting-needle points from becoming damaged, to prevent work from sliding off the needles and to stop the needle tips from piercing the workbag when stored inside.

polyester
A manufactured fiber, made from any of a group of condensation polymers. It is extremely resilient, smooth, crisp and particularly springy; it can be shaped with heat and is insensitive to moisture.

It is also lightweight, strong and resistant to creasing, shrinking, stretching, mildew and abrasion. It is readily washable, is not damaged by sunlight or weather and is resistant to moths and mildew. Polyester has many uses and is often combined with other fibers.

pompom
A fluffy ball of yarn used to decorate hats, at the ends of cords, or to make soft toys. To make a pompom you will need a pompom maker or two circles of stiff cardboard the diameter of the pompom, with a smaller hole about half this diameter through the center. Wind the yarn around the card circles through the center hole until the card is completely covered and the central hole is full. Cut through the yarn at the outside edge with a pair of sharp scissors, ease the card circles apart and tie a length of yarn between them in a firm knot to hold the yarn strands together, leaving an end to attach the pompom. Remove the circles, fluff out the pompom and trim the ends even as required. *See also* bobbles.

pongee
A natural-colored, lightweight, plain-weave, silk-like fabric with a slubbed effect.

Popcorn

A stitch in crochet that creates a firm bobble on the surface of the fabric. With right side of the work facing, make four or more stitches into the same stitch. Remove the hook from the final stitch and insert it from front to back of the first stitch. Collect the loose loop and pull through to the front. Continue along the row in the normal way. *See also* cluster, bobbles, Puff Stitch.

poplin

A heavy, plain-woven fabric with a corded surface, which was originally made with a silk warp and a worsted weft. The term is now more often used for a similar fabric made in pure cotton. It is mainly used for very high-quality shirts and blouses.

Porto Rico Rose

See Bullion Stitch/Knot.

Portuguese Knotted Stem Stitch

An embroidery stitch that creates a raised effect like a knotted rope, which can be worked in a straight line or in a circle. First work a Stem Stitch, come up at the center to one side, whip twice. Create the next stitch with the next lot of whipping going around both stitches. Repeat to end.

Post Stitch

See Bullion Stitch/Knot.

pouncing

A technique used to transfer lines and markings to fabric, traditionally used in tailoring but also for transferring embroidery designs and similar. Use a pin or the unthreaded needle in a sewing machine to make holes along the lines of a design, then pin the paper to the fabric and brush the fine pounce powder (sometimes known as inking powder) through the holes to transfer a dotted outline of the design to the fabric.

pre-shrunk

A fabric that has been shrunk before cutting so that its dimensions will not decrease further when it is laundered or dry cleaned. Many fabrics are pre-shrunk by the manufacturer.

press

Using an iron in a press/pick up and move/press motion, rather than moving it back and forth on the fabric. Pressing is done as you work, or as the final finish to a project.

press studs

UK term for snaps, a small, round fastening—one side of which has a little knob and the other a sprung hole. Press studs are also sometimes called poppers and are usually made of metal, but can also be plastic.

pressed quilts

See stitch-and-flip.

presser foot

The part of the sewing machine that holds the fabric in place as it is being sewn and fed through by the feed dogs. A variety of different feet are often included with a sewing machine or can be bought as extras. Examples include: **embroidery foot**—made of clear plastic so that you can see the work underneath it; **walking foot**—enables smoother sewing when working with several layers or fabric by providing extra hold from the top to work the feed dogs below the fabric, pushing or 'walking' the fabric; **zip/zipper foot**—a narrow foot that can slide from side to side so that you can stitch either side of it.

press piecing

See stitch-and-flip.

PRICK STITCH

Prick Stitch

A type of Backstitch used on delicate fabrics or in place of topstitching. It is worked like Backstitch, but the stitches on the front are tiny and spaced around 6mm (¼in) apart.

pricking card

A stiff card used in bobbin lacemaking, on which the pattern is marked with pinholes. The card is fastened to a firm pillow as the lace is made.

Princess Feather

A traditional type of appliqué quilt with four blocks, each of which has a design of plumed feathers rotating in a circle. It dates from the mid-18th century and may have been developed as a tribute to Victoria, Princess Royal, eldest daughter of Queen Victoria.

printed fabric

A fabric with a design printed onto the

surface, rather than woven in. As a result, the colors are usually brighter and clearer on the right side.

PUFF STITCH

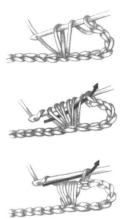

Puff Stitch

A crochet stitch that creates a smooth bump on the surface of the fabric. To work it, yarn over, insert hook into the stitch, yarn over and pull a loop through, lift hook horizontal so the loop is elongated. Pull through two more long loops, yarn over, pull through all seven loops on the hook. At the end, you can work an extra chain to close the Puff Stitch firmly. *See also* bobbles, cluster, Popcorn.

Purl Stitch

The second basic stitch in knitting. To work it, hold the needle with the stitches in the left hand with the yarn at the front, insert the tip of the right needle into the end stitch from right to left, wind the yarn from right to left over the point of the right needle and draw the yarn through the stitch, forming a new stitch on the right needle. Slip the original stitch off the left needle.

purl through back loop

A knitting technique in which the Purl Stitch is made by inserting the right needle into the back loop of the stitch instead of the front loop. This creates a firmer fabric and is often used in cable patterns to make the design more distinct. *See also* knit through back loop.

purl two together

A knitting technique in which two stitches are purled at the same time, the simplest method of decreasing. *See also* knit two together.

purlwise

Working a knitted fabric in Purl Stitch.

Quarter Stitch
See fractional stitches.

Quill Stitch
See Cretan Stitch.

quilting
A fabric construction in which a layer of batting/wadding is placed between two layers of fabric, and then held in place by stitching of some kind. If the project has no central filling, it is a coverlet, not a quilt.

Quilting Stitch
A stitch used in hand quilting, similar to an ordinary Running Stitch but much harder to work. Insert the needle through all layers of the fabric, then tilt it upwards through all the layers each time again. Take two or three stitches onto the needle before pulling the thread through. It takes a great deal of practice to create even stitches with this method.

quilt-as-you-go
A technique of quilting in which the quilt is created and quilted in one go. Cut strips of fabric to the correct width and a piece of batting/wadding about 5cm (2in) larger than the finished block. Take two strips right sides together and lay them wrong side down on the edge of the batting/wadding. Stitch along the right-hand side of the strips through all layers, then fold back the top strip and place a third strip right side down over it; stitch in place. Repeat with the other strips until the square of batting/wadding is covered.

quilter's disk
A small disk with a hole in the center used to add a seam allowance around the edge of shaped or curved templates.

Purchased templates do not usually include a seam allowance, so they are placed on the fabric and the quilter's disc is placed against an edge with a pencil or marker in the hole. The disk is rolled around the template so the pencil draws a cutting line ¼in (6mm) away from the edge.

quilter's quarter
A ¼in (6mm) ruler used to add a seam allowance to straight edges.

quilter's ruler
A very wide clear plastic ruler, available in imperial or metric, with measurements, diagonal lines at various angles and seam widths marked on it.

R

raffia
Fiber from the raffia palm, used to make craft items such as baskets, mats and hats.

railroading
A method for preventing twisting when working Cross Stitch using two threads, by bringing the needle up between the threads. It adds time but improves the appearance of the stitch and coverage.

Raised Chain Band
A composite embroidery stitch used to create a decorative band. Work a line of equally spaced horizontal Straight Stitches, then use a contrasting thread to work a line of Chain Stitch down the center, wrapping the thread around the horizontal stitch each time so that the chain is anchored on these stitches and not in the fabric.

Raised Chevron Stitch
An embroidery stitch that creates a wide, decorative band, which should be worked in quite a heavy thread for best effect. Draw three parallel lines as a guide before beginning, then work two lines of V-stitches spaced a little apart, with both rows pointing towards the center and the stitches in one row opposite the spaces in the other. With a contrasting thread, lace around one leg of a V in the upper row, over the top of the V and around the other leg, then down to repeat on the next V in the lower row. Repeat to end.

Stitch Wit
"The whole nine yards" is an expression which came from the amount of fabric needed to make fashionable coats for upper class men in England, during the early 1700s.

127

RAISED FISHBONE STITCH

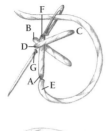

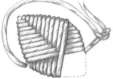

Raised Fishbone Stitch

A padded embroidery stitch used to fill motifs or to create a raised line. It is created by working diagonal stitches alternately in opposite directions, crossing the thread from one side to the other each time.

Raised Satin Stitch

See Padded Satin Stitch.

ralli

A traditional type of appliqué quilt, mainly made in the Sindh province of Pakistan but also in Rajasthan, Gujarat and the Punjab. Rallis were once made of old cloth and are generally pieced from small patches torn to the right size and sewn together by hand, with dense stitching, fine appliqué and cotton tufts for added decoration. Typical colors are red, yellow, black, and white.

ravel/unravel

A term used to describe the stitches coming undone in knitting or crochet. Sometimes used as a description of threads coming loose on fabric, which in the UK is called fraying.

raw edge

A cut edge of fabric that has not been finished in any way.

rayon

Rayon is a manufactured cellulose fiber made from viscose. It is highly absorbent, takes dye well, is soft and has a good drape. Although it has a tendency to shrink, it does not melt at high temperatures and is resistant to moths, bleach and most household chemicals. Rayon thread is divisible, shiny and good for blending, but is not particularly hardwearing.

Redwork

A type of quilting in which the blocks

are embroidered with outlines of flowers or other motifs in red thread, usually on a white background fabric. They became popular in the late 19th century, after the invention of a machine to stamp embroidery motifs on fabric, and also Turkey Red, a colorfast red dye. Any outline embroidery stitch can be used, but Redwork is usually worked in Backstitch, Stem Stitch or Chain Stitch.

REEF KNOT

Reef Knot
UK term for a knot known as Square Knot or Box Stitch in the US, and used in many needlecrafts. To make it, hold one string in each hand. Take the string in your left hand over the one in your right, round under, then over again. Then take the string now in your right hand back over the one in your left, round under, then over again. Pull gently on both sides to tighten the knot. The final knot should be perfectly symmetrical and lie flat.

reel
See spool.

reinforcing
Strengthening an area that will be subjected to strain by making extra rows of stitching or adding an underlay or a patch of fabric.

representational blocks
Blocks used in patchwork/quilting, designed to be figurative rather than geometric or abstract. They can be quite detailed or simple representative shapes and are usually pieced or appliquéd. Common designs are: **Basket block**, in which the design is a basket holding fruit or flowers; S**choolhouse** or **Housetop**, made of simple geometric shapes to indicate a house with pitched roof, chimney, two windows and a door; **Sunbonnet Sue**, showing a small child, usually wearing a print dress with a big sunbonnet.

return
In curtainmaking, this is the distance between the front face of the track and the face of the wall behind. If the track curves back to meet the wall, the return will need to be taken into account when measuring up for curtains.

129

REVERS

revers

Turned-back fabric creating shaped lapels on a jacket, coat or blouse, which can be either wide or narrow. This style of shaped lapels is sometimes also known as a rever collar or a tailored collar. *See also* flat collar, mandarin collar, Peter Pan collar, rolled collar, shawl collar.

reverse appliqué

A type of appliqué in which the design is cut out of the top layer of fabric to reveal a different layer of fabric underneath it.

Reverse Chain Stitch

This embroidery stitch, and the very similar Heavy Chain Stitch, are worked in the opposite way to normal Chain Stitch. The loop in Heavy Chain Stitch is worked twice to create a heavy chain. Reverse Chain Stitch is also known as

Broad Chain Stitch, and Heavy Chain Stitch is also known as Heavy Braid Chain Stitch.

reverse shaping

An instruction found in knitting and crochet patterns, indicating that the shaping instructions given for one side should be worked in reverse for the opposite side.

Reverse Stockinette/Stocking Stitch

See Stockinette/Stocking Stitch.

Rhodes Stitch

A raised, filling embroidery stitch used in counted-thread work. It covers a square of canvas and is worked as a series of 12 diagonal stitches spiral around the square from side to side, finished with a small vertical stitch in the center.

Ribbing/Rib

A knitting stitch often used as an edging at hem and cuffs as it creates a tight but elastic edge. The most basic form of Ribbing is worked on an even number of stitches as knit one, purl one, so on subsequent rows the knit stitch is always over the knit and vice versa, creating a line of ribs on both sides of the fabric.

Ribbing can be varied by working knit two, purl two to make wider ribs, or by working unequal numbers such as knit three, purl one.

ribbon embroidery
A type of raised embroidery that originated in France in the 18th century. Ribbons are either threaded into a needle and used instead of thread to create the stitches, couched to the background fabric, or pleated and ruched into rosettes and flowers and stitched on.

ribbon thread/floss
A type of thin ribbon specifically made for ribbon embroidery. Knitting ribbon can also be used for this type of work.

Ribbon Stitch
An embroidery stitch used specifically in ribbon embroidery, which works particularly well to create petals and leaves. The ribbon should lie flat against the fabric when the stitch has been completed, but do not pull it too tight.

Rice Stitch/Rice Grain Stitch
See Dot Stitch.

rickrack
A type of braid in a zigzag shape that is applied as a decoration. If it is stitched right at the edge of the work, it creates an attractive, scalloped edge.

right front
Normally the right section of the front of a garment, when wearing it.

right side
See wrong side.

right twist
(1) *yarn See* twist. (2) *knitting* Knitted cables and twisted stitches can twist to

RIBBON STITCH

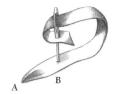
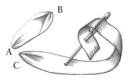

the right (counterclockwise) or to the left (clockwise). *See also* cable4back .

Rings

A basic stitch in tatting, in which chains of Double Stitches are joined into a ring. Once you have made enough Double Stitches, take the stitches and thread off your hand and pinch the first and last stitches of the ring between your index finger and thumb. Pull carefully on the thread coming from the shuttle and the ring will begin to draw up; pull until the ring closes completely, and the stitches lie flat in a neat oval with a little point at the end where the line of stitches starts and finishes.

rip

(1) To remove machine stitching. (2) To tear a piece of fabric.

rolled collar

This type of collar stands up from the neck edge, then rolls down to the rest of the garment. The curve at the neck edge of a rolled collar is less pronounced than the curve at the neck edge of the garment. *See also* flat collar, mandarin collar, Peter Pan collar, revers shawl collar.

rolled hem

A hand-stitched hem used on sheer and lightweight fabrics. The raw edge is rolled into a tiny narrow hem by hand or tucked under with the point of the needle and stitched in place with tiny Hemming Stitches. *See also* fused hem, machine-rolled hem, zigzag hemming.

Romanian Couching

An ornamental stitch for filling in areas, which has a laid thread with tying

ROLLED COLLAR

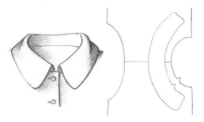

stitches set closely together over it. The laid thread and the tying stitches are worked with the same thread and it is very similar to Bokhara Couching, except the tying stitches are much closer together. *See also* Bokhara Couching, Couching.

Romanian Stitch
See Antique Stitch.

Rope Stitch
An embroidery stitch that creates a textured outline, which can be worked in tight curves as well as in a straight line. For best effect, the stitches should be worked close together to give a rope-like effect.

Rosette Chain Stitch
See Bead Edging Stitch.

rotary cutter
A tool with a rounded blade at the tip and usually an ergonomically designed and padded handle. The blade may have a pinked edging, or another design. This tool is wonderful for cutting several layers of fabric into identical straight strips. Many people also use them for curved lines and for garment pattern cutting.

rouleau loop
A narrow tube of fabric stitched in a loop in the seam at the edge of a garment, which will loop over a button to fasten the opening. Rows of rouleau loops are sometimes used as a decorative fastening down the back of dressy garments such as wedding or evening dresses. *See* bias loops.

rounds
Crochet worked in the round rather than backwards and forwards in rows. Rounds can be square or circular.

row counter
A small plastic cylinder with rotating numbered wheels, which slips onto the end of a knitting needle and can be used to keep track of rows—for instance, when decreasing and increasing. You have to remember to turn the wheel at the end of each row.

rows
When working knitting or crochet, the line of stitches or loops from one side of the piece to the other is called a row. At the end of the row, you normally reverse the needles and work back the other way. Also known as courses. *See also* wales.

ruching
Several lines of stitching, either pulled up or with shirring elastic as the bottom thread on the bobbin of the sewing maching, to form a puckered area of fabric.

ruffle
A ruffled, gathered or pleated border used to trim clothing. *See also* frill.

rug hook
A hook similar to a crochet hook, used for rug hooking, but also in knitting and crochet to pick up dropped stitches. *See also* latch hook.

rug hooking
A technique of making a rug by hand, using short lengths of yarn or strips of fabric and a rug hook to thread them through an even-weave fabric such as canvas or sacking. Latch-hooked rugs are made with a latch hook, and the yarn is knotted to secure it.

ruler
Many needlecrafts require accurate measuring to achieve good results. Tape measures can stretch in time, so for small measurements a ruler with both imperial and metric measurements is an essential piece of equipment. Plastic rulers allow you to see the material beneath, while metal rulers can also be used as a guide when cutting with a knife or rotary cutter.

RUNNING STITCH

Running Stitch
The simplest basic embroidery stitch, which consists of straight, even stitches worked at regular intervals. It is the basis of many more complex stitches, but can also be worked in rows, staggered or used as an outline to give a range of different effects.

running under
A method of securing the end of a thread before beginning to stitch by running the needle under a few threads of the fabric on the reverse before bringing it through to the front surface.

S

Saami quilt
Traditional quilts from an itinerant community living in small groups along the waterways of the Sindh province of Pakistan. They feature brightly colored fabrics, often recycled and patched old cloth, which is quilted in a limited repertoire of embroidery stitches in concentric rectangles. Sometimes there is also an embroidered right-angle shape at each corner.

sag
See drop.

salem cloth
A 100 percent machine-washable polyester cloth, often prefringed and made into finished items like sachets, bread cloths, placemats, napkins, runners, and the like. It is sometimes available by the yard/meter.

sampler
A piece of embroidery worked in a variety of stitches and motifs, designed either to practice different stitches or to show off the embroiderer's skill.

sampler quilt
A quilt worked with a variety of different blocks, either as a practice piece or to show off the needlewoman's skills.

sandpaper board
A small board covered in sandpaper, used in appliqué to hold small cut fabric elements safe before they are used.

sashiko
A form of quilting that originated in Japan, originally to hold several layers of fabric together for worker's clothing. It is worked in thick thread and with larger stitches, often in white thread on a plain blue or red background.

sashing

Horizontal and vertical strips of fabric used in quilting to space and set off the blocks, if they are not designed to be joined edge to edge.

sateen

A cotton fabric that is woven like satin with a lustrous surface and is often used for bed linens. In cheaper versions the luster is produced by pressing the fabric through rollers, but in this case the sheen disappears after several launderings so the fabric is not true sateen.

satin

A fabric either of silk or various man-made fibers, with a lustrous surface on one side produced by a twill weave with the weft threads almost hidden, and a dull back. It became known in Europe during the 12th and 13th centuries in Italy and was found in England by the 14th century, where it became a favorite for those at Court because of its excellent qualities and feel. Satin is made in many colors, weights, varieties, qualities and degrees of stiffness. It is used for lingerie, eveningwear, millinery, curtains, upholstery and as a lining fabric. *See also* crêpe-back satin.

SATIN COUCHING

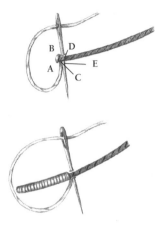

Satin Couching

A form of embroidery used particularly in goldwork, in which a base thread is laid down on the fabric and then completely covered with closely spaced Satin Stitch.

Satin Stitch

One of the basic embroidery stitches, used as a filling stitch and as the basis for a wide variety of more complex stitches. Satin Stitch is made up of a series of straight stitches worked very closely together to create a smooth surface with no fabric showing beneath. For best results, stretch the fabric on a hoop or frame to keep it taut as you work. It is also sometimes known as Damask Stitch.

Sawtooth

A patchwork pattern based on triangles in contrasting fabrics pieced to create rows of sharp points like teeth, either in the block or in the border.

Scallop Stitch

A machine stitch that creates a series of scalloped curves, either as a decorative border or to be used as an edging. If used as an edging, the stitching is done first and the fabric is then trimmed close to the stitching line. Scalloped edges can also be created with hand stitching by cutting the scallops first and then working tightly spaced Buttonhole Stitch along the edges.

Scherenschnitte

Scherenschnitte is a German word that means cutting with scissors; it has come to refer to a type of cutting in which paper is folded in quarters and cut into a design. When unfolded, a symmetrical shape is formed. The technique was adapted to make motifs in fabric to appliqué onto quilt blocks, and such quilts are known generally as Scherenschnitte quilts. *See also* Hawaiian quilts.

scissors

There are many different types of scissors, each of which is best suited to a particular purpose. Never use fabric or thread scissors to cut paper, as this will blunt the edges. Some useful types of scissors are: **dressmaker's shears**—these have angled handles to allow the blades to rest on the table as you cut and blades 7–8in (18–21cm) long; **embroidery or thread scissors**—small, sharp scissors with fine points and 3–4in (7–10 cm) blades for cutting threads, clipping seam allowances; **general purpose scissors**—medium-sized scissors for cutting paper.

Scottish knitting

See Tunisian crochet.

Knit Bit

The first knitting machine, invented in England in 1589 by William Lee, was refused a patent by Queen Elizabeth on the grounds that it would curtail the work of hand knitters.

Scottish method
See English method.

SCROLL STITCH

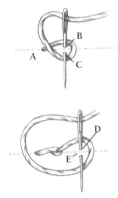

Scroll Stitch
An embroidery stitch worked from left to right to create a line of knots, which is useful as a decorative outline. Also known as Single Knotted Line Stitch.

seam
(1) *seam allowance* The amount of fabric allowed for seams when joining two pieces of fabric together. Paper patterns usually have a seam allowance of ⅝in (15mm), between the cutting line and the seamline. Templates for patchwork or motifs for appliqué may not have a seam allowance included.

(2) *seam edge* The cut edge of the seam allowance. (3) *seam line* The line that should be stitched.

seam ripper
A small tool with a very sharp, curved blade at the end, used to cut through stitches when opening a seam.

seed beads
Tiny round beads, available in both glass and plastic, in a wide range of colors and in several sizes. They are usually sold by weight and are used for jewelry and for stitched beading. They tend to be too small for knitted or crochet beading.

SEED STITCH

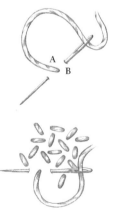

Seed Stitch

(1) *embroidery* A filling stitch, created by making tiny random Straight Stitches, usually of equal length but at contrasting angles. Also known as Speckling Stitch, Seeding Stitch. (2) *knitting* Seed Stitch, a knitted stitch pattern created by working an uneven number of stitches in alternate Knit and Purl Stitches, so in each following rows the Knit Stitch sits on top of the Purl Stitch. It creates a hard-wearing and attractive textured fabric. The UK term is Moss Stitch.

seersucker

A fabric made with a special weave so that it has lines of bunched threads giving alternate stripes of puckered finish and smooth finish. It is usually made of cotton, but sometimes synthetic, and the stripes always run lengthwise in the direction of the warp. It can be a plain color, but is often blue and white—the puckered stripes being colored and the flat ones white. Used for blouses and casual shirts.

selvage/selvedge

The finished edges on a length of woven fabric, parallel to the lengthwise threads. It often contains information from the manufacturer, such as the fabric com- position or color code. Generally, the selvage should not be incorporated into a project as it may pucker after the item has been washed.

Seminole

A type of piecing based on the work of the Seminole tribe of Native Americans in Florida. Strips of brightly colored fabric are stitched together, then cut at a 45° angle and pieced again to create chevron designs. Seminole patterns are used on skirts and bags, and although not usually used for entire quilts they can make wonderfully intricate borders.

separating zipper/zip

A zipper that comes completely apart when unzipped. There is a special tab at the bottom of a separating zipper for bringing it together and starting the zipper. Also known as open-ended zipper. *See also* concealed zipper, fly front zipper, lapped zipper.

sequins

Small pieces of mirrored material made of metal or plastic, usually round, with a central hole for stitching or threading. Sequins come in a range of sizes and shapes, flat or faceted. They are used in sewing, knitting, and crochet.

serger

A type of sewing machine that stitches the seam, encases the seam with thread, and cuts off excess fabric at the same time. They are mainly used to make garments in knit fabric, or to finish seams of any fabric. Some sergers are combination overlock and serger machines. They do not, however, do the basic straight stitching or any of the decorative effects that a regular sewing machine does.

shade

Yarn and thread not only come in different colors but also different shades—for instance, there may be several different reds or blues. Different shades of yarn are indicated on the ball band by a shade number, sometimes also with a color name. Shades of thread are also differentiated by a number, name, or both, on the end of the spool or on the wrapper.

shadow quilting

A form of quilting in which the design is created in very bright fabrics, a transparent fabric is laid over the top and then the piece is quilted through all layers to create a muted effect.

shadowwork

An embroidery technique using sheer fabric with only the barest outline of the pattern on the surface. The criss-crossed threads underneath show through the fabric, creating a shadow pattern. It is the opacity of threads worked on sheer fabric that defines this form of embroidery, rather than any single stitch or color combination.

shank

The stem between the back of a button and the surface of the fabric. Can be part of the button or made of thread when the button is stitched on. It allows room for the layers of fabric on the buttonhole side when the button is done up.

sharkskin

A hard-finished, low-luster, medium-weight fabric in a twill weave. It is most commonly used for men's suits, but it can also be found in a plain weave of acetate, triacetate and rayon, which is used for women's sportswear.

shawl collar

A long collar folding down the front of a garment, with one side overlapping the other. *See also* flat collar, mandarin collar, Peter Pan collar, rolled collar.

SHEAF STITCH

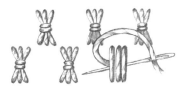

Sheaf Stitch

A filling embroidery stitch, which consists of three vertical Satin Stitches tied across the center with two horizontal stitches, worked either in rows or randomly spaced. The horizontal stitches should only go around the Satin Stitches and not into the fabric.

sheer

(1) A fabric that is semi-transparent. (2) Sheers is a general term used in the UK for semi-transparent curtains.

shirring

Gathering with three or more parallel rows of stitching to control fullness. Shirring elastic can be put on the bobbin of a sewing machine to gather large areas of fabric in this way, which will give to fit closely around the body.

shisha mirror

Small pieces of reflective mica used in embroidery and attached to fabric with a special stitch, which covers the edges entirely leaving a round mirror showing.

short-row shaping

A technique in knitting, sometimes also called turning rows, in which shaping is carried out within the piece without binding/casting off any stitches until all the shaping is complete. It is often used to shape collars or shoulders on a fitted garment. On a knit row, work to the turning point, slip the next stitch purlwise with yarn at back, bring the yarn forward between the needles, slip the stitch back to the left needle and take the yarn to the back through the needles, turn and work to the end. Continue in this way until the shaping is complete.

shoulder length measurement

Measurement from the base of the neck to the point of the shoulder. To find the shoulder point, raise the arm to shoulder height; the dimple that forms on top marks the shoulder point.

shuttle

A tatting shuttle is normally a metal or plastic pointed oval shape less than 3in

(7cm) long, although shuttles come in a variety of shapes and materials, often with a point or hook at one end. To make the lace, the tatter wraps the thread around one hand and manipulates the shuttle with the other hand. *See also* Double Stitch, Picot, Rings, tatting.

sides to middle

Folding the two selvage edges of a fabric to meet at the centerline. This is used when a lot of the pattern pieces need to be placed on a fold line. At one time, a worn double sheet would be stitched sides to middle to get more wear out of it as a single sheet.

silk

A natural filament fiber produced by the silkworm in the construction of its cocoon. Most silk is collected from cultivated worms and all silk comes from Asia, primarily China. Silk is one of the finest textiles; it is soft, has a brilliant sheen and is very strong and absorbent. It is one of the oldest known textile fibers—according to Chinese tradition, it was used as long ago as 2700 BC. The silkworm moth was originally a native of China and for about 3000 years the gathering and weaving of silk was a secret process, known only to the Chinese. There are several types of silk, including: **dupioni**—yarn made from the cocoon of two silk worms that have nested together; the double strand is not separated so the yarn is uneven and irregular with a large diameter in places and the fabric is plain weave, very irregular and shows many slubs; **raw/wild/tussah/shantung silk**—a thicker, shorter fiber produced by worms in their natural habitat; **shot silk**—woven with the warp and weft in different colors, giving a different effect when viewed from different angles. *See also* habotai, noil, tussah.

silk pins

Very fine, sharp pins used when working with silk fabrics, often with a small glass pearl bead at the top.

SINGLE CROCHET (US)

Single Crochet

A crochet stitch that in the UK is called Double Crochet. *See also* Double Crochet.

Single Knotted Line Stitch

See Scroll Stitch.

sisal

The fiber from sisal, a Mexican agave plant, used for craftwork, mattings and rope.

size

The size given on a pattern may not correspond with ready-to-wear garments, as each manufacturer has their own set of standard measurements. Always check the actual measurements in order to be sure that the pattern will need as little alteration as possible. There is nothing to stop you making the top half of a garment in one size and the bottom in another, or knitting sleeves for one size and the body in another if this means the item will fit you better—as long as you remember to allow for and adjust where the two sections will join.

sizing

A finish applied to fabric to add body and stiffness. It can be removed by laundering.

skein

A skein is a ⅙ of a hank. The length of a skein varies for each type of fiber and manufacturer. Guide lengths are: stranded cotton 8¾yd (8m); tapestry wool 10yd (9m); and crewel wool 33yd (30m).

skip

Term for going past a stitch or a row in knitting or crochet without working it. UK term is miss.

skirt length

The measurement from waist to hem of a skirt or the skirt section of a dress. It can be any length to suit the individual, but there are a range of set lengths: **floor length,** with the hem touching the floor; **maxi** or **ankle** length, with the hem an inch or so off the floor; **midi** or **mid-calf**, with the hem falling midway between knee and ankle; **knee-length**, on the knee; **mini**, above the knee.

skirt marker

A tool for marking the length of a skirt so that the hem can be stitched. There are two types available: the **pin marker**, which requires a second person to place the pins, and the **chalk marker**, which has a bulb with chalk dust and can be operated by the person wearing the skirt.

slash
A cut in fabric along a straight line, but longer than a clip.

slashed quilting
A type of quilting in which the layers of fabric are quilted together with an extra top layer, sometimes only in some areas, which is slashed between the stitches to show the base fabric beneath.

sleeves
There are many different designs of sleeve and they make a big difference to how the final garment will look. Some styles are: **kimono sleeve**—cut as part of the front and back of the garment; **leg-of-mutton sleeve**—a sleeve with a full top, but which fits tightly from elbow to wrist; **puff sleeve**—full at the shoulder, but gathered in at the top of the arm; **raglan sleeve**—joined to the body with a diagonal seam from collar to underarm; **set-in sleeve**—fit into the armhole of the front and back.

sleeveboard
A piece of equipment used when pressing narrow sections of garments, particularly sleeves. It is usually in the shape of a miniature shaped and padded board that sits on top of the main ironing surface on a cantilevered base. *See also* ham, needleboard.

KIMONO SLEEVE

LEG-O-MUTTON SLEEVE

SLIP KNOT

slip one knitwise

A knitting technique to go past a stitch without working it. To slip a stitch knitwise, insert the tip of the right needle as if to knit, then slip the stitch onto the right needle.

slip one purlwise

A knitting technique to go past a stitch without working it. To pass a stitch purlwise, insert the tip of the right needle as if to purl, then slip the stitch onto the right needle.

SLIP STITCH

slip knot

The first stitch made to begin a piece of knitting or crochet. It is formed by making a loop in the yarn, and then making a second loop and passing it through the first. This creates a loop that can be tightened on the hook or needle by pulling on the yarn end.

slip one, knit one, pass slipped stitch over

A technique for decreasing by one stitch in knitting. To work it, slip a stitch knitwise from the right to the left needle, Knit the next stitch, then lift the slipped stitch over the knit stitch and off the needle.

Slip Stitch

One of the basic stitches in crochet, which is used to join chains into a ring. Insert the hook into the stitch, yarn over hook, draw the thread through both loops on the hook.

Slipstitch

A stitch worked with a yarn needle, used to join seams in knitting and crochet.

Thread the needle with matching yarn, and lay the pieces edge to edge. Bring the needle through the main piece from the back, picking up a bar from the center of a stitch. From the front, pick up a bar from a stitch of the second piece. Continue in this way until the seam is complete. *See also* Backstitch, Mattress Stitch.

slipstitch selvage

A technique of finishing an edge in knitting. Slip the first stitch of each row, making sure to slip knitwise on a knit row and purlwise on a purl row. This technique gives a neat edge, but can cause problems if stitches need to be picked up on the edge later. Also known as chain selvedge.

Slip Basting/Tacking

A technique used in dressmaking/tailoring to match stripes or checks, or join intricate curved sections. Working from the right side, fold the seam allowance under on one edge and pin or baste/tack. Lap this edge over the seam allowance of the other piece, carefully matching each strip or check, and hold in place with pins at right angles to the fold. Using contrasting thread, bring a needle up from the wrong side through three layers of fabric at the edge of the fold, then take the needle back down directly opposite through a single thickness of fabric. This will create a long stitch on the underside and a short stitch under the folded edge. When finished, remove the pins and machine stitch the seam as usual, through the center of the tacking/basting stitches, which can then be removed.

slit

(1) A small elongated cut in a piece of fabric. *See also* slash, snip. (2) A finished opening in a garment, either for ease of movement, such as in the hem of a skirt, or for decorative effect. *See also* placket.

sloper

A basic pattern, from which other designs can be developed. It has no style of its own, but is fitted, with a minimum ease allowance, and can be used to work out where standard patterns need to be adjusted to fit.

slub

An uneven thread or yarn with thicker sections, which may be accidental or by design. When woven the fabric will have random nubs running with the weave.

With some fabrics, such as slubbed silk, this is part of the character of the fabric.

smocking
A traditional form of embroidery in which the fabric is gathered into a series of even, decorative folds. It is usually used on yokes, sometimes also on cuffs, and creates a slightly elastic fabric. *See also* Cable Stitch, Diamond Stitch (smocking), Honeycomb Stitch.

Smyrna Stitch
A knotted embroidery stitch that is often used in Italian embroidery, particularly for outlines. It creates a knotted line that is easy to work around quite complex shapes. Also known as Double Knot Stitch, Old English Knot Stitch, Palestrina Stitch, Tied Coral Stitch.

Snail Trail
See Beaded Stitch.

snaps
A small, round fastening, one side of which has a little knob and the other a sprung hole. Snaps are usually of made of metal, but can also be plastic. The UK term is press studs or poppers.

snip
A short cut in a piece of fabric. *See also* clip, slash.

spacer bar
A small strip of metal punched with spaced holes, used in beading to keep rows of a necklace apart.

spacer blocks
Blocks usually made in plain fabric and used in quilting to separate the main design blocks or to fill in the spaces left—such as when working with octagonal blocks, which can only be stitched together on the vertical and horizontal edges and so require square blocks on point to fill in around them.

spandex
See elastane.

Spanish Coral Stitch
See Crested Chain Stitch.

Spanish Knotted Feather Stitch
See Twisted Zigzag Chain Stitch.

Speckling Stitch
See Seed Stitch.

Spider Web Rose

An embroidery stitch used in ribbon embroidery, which is created by stitching five straight stitches like the spokes of a wheel, then weaving narrow ribbon over and under them in a circle to create a small, raised rose.

SPIDER WEB STITCH

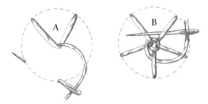

Spider Web Stitch

A type of embroidery stitch made up of a Fly Stitch and two Straight Stitches to create five spokes of a wheel. The thread is then woven over and under the spokes to create a filled circle. In drawn-thread embroidery, the spokes are sometimes only half filled with weaving, creating a more open effect.

spiral

See twist.

Split Rings

A stitch used in tatting, in which the ring is made in two halves. To make Split Rings in shuttle tatting you normally need two shuttles, one for each half of the ring. In needle tatting you work the first half of the ring in the regular manner, then unthread your needle, turn it around and work the other half of your ring with the thread that went through the needle's eye. The first half is worked towards the tip of the needle, and the second half towards the eye. When you reach the end, re-thread your needle and close the ring as usual.

Split Stitch

See Kensington Outline Stitch.

spool

(1) The small tube that holds the thread, also known as a reel. It can be made of wood, plastic, or cardboard. Cone spools, as the name suggests, are cone-shaped. (2) Another term for a French knitting doll/dolly.

spool knitting

See French knitting.

sportweight

A mediumweight yarn, which is heavier than 4-ply (fingering) but lighter than Aran. It is also sometimes called sport.

In the UK, it is called double-knitting yarn.

square brackets
These are used in knitting/crochet patterns to indicate groups of stitches that are to be repeated, with the number of repeats indicated after them.

Square Knot
See Reef Knot.

St George's Cross Stitch
An embroidery stitch that is worked as a Cross Stitch standing on one leg to form a plus or addition sign. It can be worked in rows or scattered randomly across an area.

Stab Stitch
A stitch used in quilting and embroidery in which the needle and thread are taken through the layers of fabric at the perpendicular and in only one direction at a time.

stamped cross stitch
A fabric with a design printed on it in different colors, ready for Cross Stitch to be worked over the top. This means that there is no need to count threads as you work.

stand pocket
A type of inset pocket that is used on tailored garments, particularly for the breast pocket of a man's jacket. It consists of two parts—the stand, a narrow band that finishes the opening and is the only part visible; and the pocket itself, or pouch, which is inside the garment, between the outside material and the lining.

standing collar
See mandarin collar.

Star Filling Stitch
A composite embroidery stitch formed by making a St George's Cross Stitch topped with a normal Cross Stitch, with all the arms of equal length. It is used to fill areas, either in rows, scattered randomly or arranged in a regular grid.

STAR STITCH

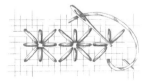

Star Stitch
An embroidery stitch used in Hardanger and drawn-thread embroidery, which

forms a square stitch over an equal number of horizontal and vertical threads. It is worked in eight Straight Stitches, two horizontal, two vertical and four diagonal, each worked into the same central hole.

star block
A pieced patchwork block used in quilting. There are many star designs. Examples include: **Four-point Star**— a star often made of four diamonds or eight pieced triangles; **Star of Bethlehem/Lone Star**—an eight-pointed star, which is made of eight diamonds often pieced from smaller elements; **Mariner's Compass**—one of the most complex star designs, with 32 or more points.

starting chain
Also called the foundation chain. The initial chain stitches made at the beginning of a crochet project as the base on which the first row or round is worked. To make chain, start with a slip knot on the hook, bring the yarn over the hook from back to front, and pull through the loop on the hook to make one chain. Continue to make the number of chains specified.

stash
A collection of fabric— either oddments left over from finished projects or pieces bought to use at some future date.

stay
A small length of tape or fabric sewn to the reverse of a garment for reinforcement – for example, at the point of a slash.

stay stitching
A line of stitching within the seam allowance and through only a single thickness of fabric. It is used to hold stretch fabrics or curved lines, such as a neckline, in their original shape and prevent them from stretching as the garment is fitted.

STEM STITCH

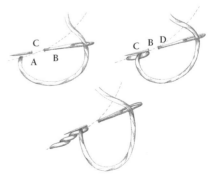

Stem Stitch

One of the basic embroidery stitches, which dates back to ancient times. It is used to outline motifs and to create the stems of leaves and flowers. When worked correctly, there should be a neat row of Backstitch on the reverse. Keep the stitches even and be sure to keep the working thread below the needle.

stencil

A shape with a line design cut in it, usually made from translucent plastic so that you can move it across and line it up to repeat the design across the fabric. Stencils are used in quilting to mark quilt stitch lines and sometimes in embroidery for stitching lines.

Step Stitch

See Ladder Stitch.

STITCH AND PINK

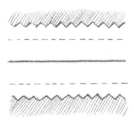

stitch and pink

A technique for seams in which a line of stitching is made within the seam allowance ¼in (6mm) from the raw edge, and the edge is then pinked near the stitching line. It is best for fabrics that do not fray or ravel easily. Also known as pinked seam.

stitch holder

A piece of equipment used in knitting that looks like a large safety pin, used to hold stitches that are not being worked secure until they are required.

stitch length/width

The length of the stitch can be adjusted on a sewing machine by changing how far the fabric is moved through the feed dogs between stitches. Different lengths are used for different functions: large stitches (4 or more) are less secure and are used for temporary stitching and gathering; shorter stitches (around 2–3) are used for seams; very short stitches (less than 2) are used for decorative effects such as top stitching. Stitch width, which is the distance the needle moves from side to side while stitching, can also be adjusted. Different combinations of width and length give a variety of effects, from an open zigzag to a tight satin-stitch look.

stitch marker
See place marker.

stitch-and-flip
A quilting technique in which a piece of fabric is placed right side up at the center of the fabric or batting/wadding foundation, and another piece placed on top, right side down. Stitch to join the two pieces, then fold the second piece over so it is right side up. Repeat with another piece of fabric, continuing until the foundation is covered. Also known as pressed quilts, press piecing.

stitch-in-the-ditch
See in-the-ditch quilting

Stockinette Stitch
One of the basic stitches in knitting, created by working Knit and Purl Stitches on alternate rows. The front of the fabric is a smooth series of V-shaped stitches, while the reverse looks like rows of ridges. Reverse Stockinette Stitch is worked in exactly the same way, but the ridged side is the right side. Known in the UK as Stocking Stitch. *See also* Garter Stitch.

stopper bead
A bead at the end of a row of beading that is held in a loop of thread to stop the other beads from sliding off.

straight grain
(1) *fabric* The straight of grain runs parallel to the selvage of a fabric. Since it lines up with the warp yarns exactly, there is little give if the fabric is pulled along the straight grain. (2) *dressmaking/tailoring* Pattern pieces often have a straight grain line marked on them. When pinning the piece to the fabric, make sure that this line is parallel to the selvedge along its length.

Straight Stitch
(1) *sewing* A row of simple, straight stitches spaced a little apart. Straight Stitch can be used to finish the edges of seams on knit fabrics. (2) *embroidery* Another term for Satin Stitch worked as single separate stitches.

stranded cotton
A divisible thread made of double mercerized long cotton fibers. Stranded cotton usually has six strands.

stranding
When knitting Fair Isle designs in several colors, you will need to carry the unused yarn across the back of the work

until it is needed again. If it is carried over more than a few stitches, it should be caught into the knitting every three or four stitches. Also known as carrying yarn. *See also* weaving.

stretch fabric seam

When sewing seams on stretch fabric, the seam needs to give a little with the fabric or the stitches will break. This can be accomplished in two ways: stitch a plain seam, stretching the fabric slightly as you sew; or stitch the seam with a narrow zigzag. To stabilize a seam on stretch fabric where it should not stretch—such as at the neckline or shoulder—stitch a length of plain tape to the seam on the inside.

strip quilt

A type of quilt with alternate stripes of contrasting colors, or patterned and plain fabric, running from one end to the other. The quilting design on these usually runs down the stripes.

stuffed quilting

See trapunto.

stumpwork

A type of embroidery that was particularly popular in the 15th and 16th centuries, in which padding was used to create three-dimensional effects.

suede

See leather.

surah

A soft, twill-weave fabric of silk or rayon, often in a plaid design or a printed pattern. It is used for ties, scarves, blouses and dresses.

Surgeon's Knot

A knot used in many types of needlecraft, for which you need an end plus a cut length of thread. To make it, hold one thread in each hand. Take the thread in your left hand over the one in your right, around under, then over again. Then take the thread now in your right hand back over the one in your left, around under, then over again. Finally, take the two ends to your left and thread them both around and up through the central loop again. Pull gently on both sides to tighten the knot.

swatch

A small piece of fabric, which is used as a color sample.

Swiss darning

Also known as Duplicate Stitch. An embroidery technique on knitted fabrics, where the knitted stitch is duplicated in a contrasting yarn so it looks as if the motif has been knitted into the fabric. Worked on Stockinette Stitch.

SWORD EDGING STITCH

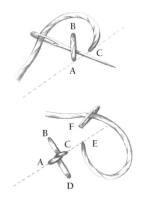

Sword Edging Stitch

An embroidery stitch that can either be worked in rows or scattered randomly across an area. It is worked by taking a short Straight Stitch diagonally up from a marked line, coming up through the fabric to the right of the base, and looping the thread around the stitch already formed to pull it back down along the line.

synthetic thread

Any type of thread that is not made of a natural fiber, such as nylon bead threads, metallic-effect thread, monofilament, polyester thread.

T

tacking

UK term for basting. A technique used to temporarily hold layers of fabric together for fitting or to stop them from slipping as seams are stitched. It is traditionally done with large, single-thread stitches, but – particularly in quilting—can also be done with pins, safety pins, basting spray or plastic ties from a basting gun.

take-up lever

A lever, usually on the front of a sewing machine, with an eye or loop that is used to guide the thread when threading the machine and moves up and down in synchronization with the action of the needle. When the take-up lever is at its highest point, the needle will be up and out of the fabric.

taffeta

A smooth, closely woven fabric in a plain weave, originally made of silk but now often of man-made fibers. It may be a solid color, have a different color warp and weft, to produce iridescence—which is sometimes called shot taffeta—or be printed or have a moiré pattern. It is used for dresses, suits, coats and lingerie.

TAILORED PLACKET

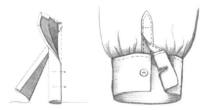

tailored placket

A type of finish to a placket at a cuff or neckline used on tailored garments, in which the edges of the placket are bound with two separate pieces of fabric,

155

which overlap and are edge stitched. The overlapping top piece is often pointed or rounded at the top where it extends past the opening. *See also* continuous bound placket, faced placket.

TAILOR'S BUTTONHOLE STITCH

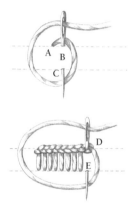

Tailor's Buttonhole Stitch
A variation on basic Buttonhole Stitch, which creates a knotted edge and is very suitable for heavyweight fabrics.

tailor's chalk
A piece of chalk used to mark construction or fitting lines on the fabric as the garment is fitted on a tailor's dummy or on the body. It is sometimes in a flat triangular shape with rounded corners, or comes in a holder with a built-in brush.

tailor's tacks
Markings in thread used to transfer symbols from the pattern to the fabric. A tailor's tack is usually a stitch taken through both thicknesses of fabric, leaving a large loop of thread on one side. When you snip the loop and remove the pattern, the pieces of fabric can be eased apart and the threads snipped between them, leaving a few strands of thread to mark the place in each piece of fabric.

tambour work
A technique of applying beading to fabric using a small hook and generally working in Chain Stitch.

tapestry
Tapestry designs are created by weaving the fabric itself rather than by stitching designs onto an openweave canvas. The origins go back well over a thousand years, coming to Europe via the Middle East. The great age of tapestry was in the 1600s and 1700s, especially in France. Hand looms gave way to power looms in the 19th century. Many of the designs from that period have retained their

popularity for needlepoint kits. The term tapestry is now often used to refer to needlepoint.

tapestry wool

A non-divisible, 4-ply wool, which is good for tapestry and canvas work.

tartan

UK term for plaid, a twill-weave cloth, usually made of wool, with alternating stripes and bands of color woven into or dyed onto the fabric. This makes blocks of color that repeat vertically and horizontally in a pattern of squares and lines. Many tartan designs are associated with a particular Scottish clan.

tassel

A tuft of loose, hanging threads or cords, knotted or bound at one end, used to decorate garments, soft furnishings and curtain cords.

tatting

Tatting is made up of Double Stitches (ds) formed along a base thread in the shape of either Rings (R) or Chains (C). These Rings and Chains are joined together by Picots (p). Picots are also used as a decorative element in the tatting design. The thread is guided on its path with a shuttle or a tatting needle. Shuttle- and needle-tatted lace look almost identical, but they differ in structure. Shuttle tatting is tighter and finer, while needle tatting can appear thick and loose because both needle and thread pass through the stitches. *See also* Chain (tatting), Double Stitch, Picot, Split Rings.

tatting needle

A tatting needle is a long needle that remains the same thickness at the eye of the needle. The needle used must match the thickness of the thread chosen for the project.

t-bar clasp

A type of clasp used in jewelry making that is easy to fasten with only one hand, so is ideal for bracelets. It consists of a metal cross bar on one side, which threads through a circle on the other and pulls straight to catch against the sides of the circle.

tear-away stabilizer

Tear-away stabilizer is used in embroidery to hold the fabric firm while it is being worked. When the design is complete, the stabilizer can be torn away carefully and removed. It is available in several weights and can be used in single or double layers. *See also* water-soluble stabilizer.

template

A shaped piece of firm but flexible material such as plastic, cardboard or heavy paper used as a pattern for marking an appliqué or patchwork design on fabric. Templates can be purchased or made, sometimes with the seam allowances included.

tension

(1) *sewing* The degree of tightness or looseness of the top (needle) and bottom (bobbin) threads on a sewing machine. The two threads should interlock in the middle, not on the top or the bottom of the fabric. (2) *knitting/crochet* UK term for the number of stitches and rows that should be achieved in a given square of fabric, to obtain the sizes given in the pattern. US term is gauge. If the maker works to a different tension, it can be adjusted by changing the size of the needles/hook used.

tension dial

The dial on a sewing machine that adjusts the tension of the upper thread, to create a perfectly locked stitch with

the two threads drawn into the fabric to the same degree. To adjust the tension of the lower thread, there is a small screw on the bobbin case or shuttle.

TENT STITCH

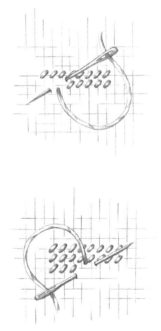

Tent Stitch

An embroidery stitch worked on even-weave fabric consisting of rows of small diagonal stitches worked from left to right, and back again on the following row. Also known as petit point.

tester

A tester bed, often also known as a four-poster, has a flat "ceiling" of fabric—or sometimes wood—that covers the entire bed area and is supported by full-height posts that extend upwards from each corner of the bed. Sometimes this type of bed also has curtains that can be drawn right around to enclose the bed. A half-tester has a "ceiling" that extends only partway down the bed and is usually cantilevered above the head end, so the bed does not have full-height foot posts. *See also* canopy.

thigh measurement

Take the thigh measurement around the fullest part of the thigh, usually towards the top of the leg.

thimble

A thimble is a protective cap for the middle finger, used when doing hand sewing. It can be made of leather, metal, wood, ceramic or other material and should fit well—not so loose that it slips off, but not so tight that it is snug. A thimble is worn on the hand that is using the needle.

Thorn and Briar Stitch

An embroidery stitch that is a variation of basic Feather Stitch. It is worked downwards and creates a pretty, feathery border. Also known as Double Feather Stitch, Double Coral Stitch.

thread

The fiber used for sewing, which comes in many different materials—including silk, cotton, polyester and blends—and is made specifically for different uses. Machine thread is usually stronger than hand-sewing thread. Some threads, such as embroidery thread and stranded cotton, are stranded and can be divided for finer work. *See also* basting thread, coton à broder, cotton perlé, crewel wool, embroidery thread, flower thread, holographic thread, metallic thread.

thread count

See count.

thread loop

A loop of thread used to catch around a button, or with a hook instead of a metal eye. Thread loops are made by stitching a few long stitches very close together, then working Buttonhole Stitch around all of them from one end to the other to make a solid thread bar.

Threaded Backstitch

A simple embroidery stitch used mainly for outlining. It consists of a line of Backstitch that has a thread woven in and out one way then back again the other way and can be worked in one, two or three colors.

Threaded Detached Chain Stitch

An embroidery stitch that can be worked in a straight line or around in tight curves. It consists of a row of single Chain Stitches spaced apart, woven through with contrasting threads one way and then the other.

THREADED HERRINGBONE STITCH

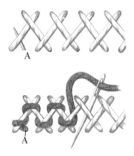

Threaded Herringbone Stitch

Another woven embroidery stitch that is useful as a wide, decorative border. Work a line of Herringbone Stitch, then weave through the stitches in a contrasting thread.

three needle cast/bind off

A knitting technique used to join two pieces of knitting while casting/binding both pieces off. It can be used only where both pieces have the same number of stitches. Hold both needles with the stitches on in your left hand, with right sides together and the needles pointing in the same direction. With a third needle in your right hand, insert the tip into the back of the stitch on the front needle and the front of the stitch on the back needle. Knit the two stitches together, then knit the next two in the same way. With the tip of one of the needles in your left hand, lift the first stitch over the second and off the third needle. Continue in this way to the end.

Three-quarter Stitch

See fractional stitches.

through back loop

See knit through back loop, purl through back loop.

thumb cast on

A technique of casting on that creates a very elastic edge. Leaving about 2in

(5cm) of yarn for each stitch to be cast on, make a slip knot and place it on the needle. With the needle and the ball of yarn in your right hand, wrap the loose end of yarn around the thumb of your left hand, from back to front. Insert the tip of the needle into the loop on your thumb, take the yarn in your right hand forwards over the tip of the needle, and draw the yarn back through the loop to make a stitch on the needle. Repeat to create as many stitches as are required. *See also* cable cast on, chain cast on, invisible cast on, long-tail cast on, picot cast on.

ticking

A thick, closely woven, twill fabric in linen or cotton, with stripes created by colored and natural or white yarns repeated in the warp, and all natural or white for the weft. There are several common color combinations, such as blue and white, brown and white, or red and white. Ticking was traditionally used for covering mattresses or for upholstery.

Tied Coral Stitch

See Smyrna Stitch.

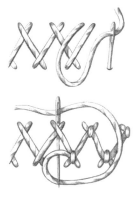

Tied Herringbone Stitch

This is an embroidery stitch worked as a line of Herringbone Stitch with Coral Stitch worked over the top in a contrasting thread. It can be used as a border or worked in rows to fill an area. Also known as Coral Knotted Herringbone Stitch.

toggle

A short rod of wood or plastic with a turned groove around the center. It is used as a fastening, by fixing it to one side of an opening by a length of cord or stitching around the groove, and threading it through a loop of cord or frogging on the other side.

toile colbert
See aida.

toile de Jouy
A type of light-colored fabric, usually cotton, printed with a design of landscape, figures or flowers. It was first made at Jouy-en-Josas, near Paris in 1759. Within a few years, the factory was the biggest of its kind in Europe and some 30,000 designs were created, many of them the work of renowned 18th-century artists such as Fragonard and Boucher.

top stitching
A decorative row of stitching on the right side of a garment, as near as possible to a finished edge—for instance, along the edge of revers. Top stitching can be done by hand or by machine. Hand stitches used include: **Glove Stitch**—small, even stitches on both sides of the material; **Saddle Stitch**— longer stitches on top and shorter beneath.

tracing wheel
Used with special tracing paper, which is placed on the fabric "ink" side down. The pattern markings to be transferred are placed on the paper and then traced over with the wheel. The wheel itself looks a bit like a pizza cutter with spikes. Care needs to be taken not to press too hard and cut the pattern, tracing paper, or the fabric. Tracing ink does not always wash out, so it may not be suitable for some types of marking.

TRAILING STITCH

Trailing Stitch
An embroidery stitch used mainly for creating a firm, raised outline. Work a row of Backstitch around the shape, then go around again wrapping the thread around the Backstitch closely together without picking up the background fabric. Also known as Whipped Backstitch.

TRAMMING

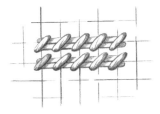

tramé/tramme/tramming

A technique in which the canvas is marked out with horizontal lines of wool, which are then overstitched with Continental Tent Stitch to give raised areas. It is excellent for hard-wearing chair covers and commonly used on duo canvas to define designs and colors accurately. Tramé dates back to medieval times, but the world center today for this work is Madeira in Portugal.

trapunto

A type of quilting in which parts of the quilting pattern are stuffed from the back to create raised areas on the surface of the quilt. Also known as stuffed quilting.

Treble Crochet

(1) US term for a crochet stitch that in the UK is called Double Treble. *See also* Double Crochet. (2) UK term for a crochet stitch that in the US is called Double Crochet.

Trellis Couching

See Jacobean Laidwork.

Triangle and Diamond Blocks

Triangle and diamond shapes have always been very popular for pieced quilting, since they add a complex new dimension to the work. As well as adding to the design possibilities, they also test the stitcher's skill, since keeping geometric shapes correct is more tricky when sewing seams on the bias. Some popular patterns made with triangular blocks include: **Lady of the Lake**—in which square blocks made of two pieced triangles are surrounded on all four sides by a Sawtooth edge; **Ocean Waves**—in which tiny blue and white triangles are pieced into a diagonal grid with plain white spacer blocks. Some typical blocks made with diamonds include: **Tumbling Blocks**—in which three diamonds are pieced together in a hexagon to create a "three-dimensional"-looking cube; **Star blocks**—in which the star is made of four or more diamonds.

tricot écossais

See Tunisian crochet.

trim/trimming

(1) Any decorative item, ribbon or lace that is put on a garment or craft item that is being sewn. (2) Used to define the act of trimming excess seam allowances or fabric with scissors.

Trip Around the World

A method of setting blocks of any shape in quilting so that the rows of color radiate out from the center. Also known as Sunshine and Shadow—particularly in Amish quilts, perhaps because they do not travel much.

Triple Treble

A type of crochet stitch. To make, bring yarn over hook four times. Insert hook into eighth chain from hook. Bring yarn over and draw yarn through stitch. Bring yarn over and draw through two loops on hook. Repeat last step four more times to complete stitch. In the UK, it is known Quadruple Treble.

tuck

A stitched fold of fabric, either as a decorative feature or to hold extra fabric in place until needed. *See also* pin tuck.

tulle

A lightweight, extremely fine, machine-made netting, usually with a hexagon-shaped mesh. End uses include dance costumes and veils.

Tunisian crochet

Tunisian crochet, also known as Afghan crochet or tricot écossais (Scottish knitting), starts with a slip knot followed by a chain like normal crochet, but the loops are picked up in one direction and removed in the other and the work is never turned. This type of crochet creates a dense fabric with a definite front and back side. It is worked by first making a starting chain, then working the first row by inserting the hook in the second chain, picking up the top strand only, yarn over hook, draw through, insert hook in the next chain without working the loop off the hook. At the end of the row, you will have one loop on the hook for each chain. Yarn over, pull through one loop, yarn over, pull through two loops. Repeat to end of row.

turkey red

A type of red fabric dye, the first to be colorfast, which made red fabric hugely popular for making quilts in the latter half of the 19th century.

TURNED AND STITCHED SEAM

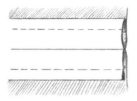

turned and stitched seam

A method of finishing off a seam in which the raw edges are turned under by up to ¼in (6mm) and stitched close to the fold. Not suitable for very heavy fabrics.

tussah

A plain-weave fabric with a rib effect formed by slub weft yarns. It is made of cotton, silk, rayon and other manmade fibers and is low in luster, heavier and rougher than pongee. Tussah is sometimes used to describe a heavy grade of pongee made in China. Also known as nankeen, rajah, and shantung. *See also* silk.

tweed

Tweed is a term broadly applied to a range of sturdy fabrics made of the coarser grades of wool, usually with color effects created by mixing stock-dyed wools, or sometimes in a single color with an interesting weave. The most popular weaves for tweeds are plain, twill, and variations of twill such as herringbone. Tweed is now also made of fibers other than wool.

tweeding

Working embroidery with two or more colors of thread in the needle.

Twist

(1) *knitting* A technique in which a line of Knit Stitches is twisted over a reverse Stockinette Stitch fabric. It is worked without a cable needle, by missing a stitch, working the next one, and then going back to work the missed stitch before slipping the worked stitch off the needle. Both stitches are then slipped off together. (2) *yarn/thread* A yarn will either have an "S" or a "Z" twist depending on how the yarn is spun: clockwise (S) or counterclockwise (Z). (3) *lacemaking* One of the basic movements in bobbin lacemaking. All the stitches involve four threads on two pairs of bobbins, which are crossed and twisted to create the stitch. To make the twist, take the right-hand threads of each pair and twist them right thread over left. The twist is always made this way.

Twist Stitch
See Long-armed/legged Cross Stitch.

twisted cord
A cord made by twisting strands of yarn. Take as many strands of yarn as required and cut them to two or three times the desired length of the final cord. Knot the strands together at each end, then attach one end to a hook or door handle and insert a knitting needle or similar in the other end. Twist the needle until the strands are tightly twisted together. The tighter the twist, the firmer the cord will be—but this will also reduce the length further. Hold the twisted cord in the center and free both ends, allowing them to twist together, then smooth the twist out so that it is even. If you use different-colored strands, you will get a diagonally striped cord.

Twisted Insertion Stitch
See Faggoting.

Twisted Zigzag Chain Stitch
A knotted embroidery stitch worked downwards to create a narrow band of twisted and knotted loops on either side of a center line, which looks like braiding. Draw three parallel lines as a guide before you start. Also known as Spanish Knotted Feather Stitch.

2-ply
A lightweight yarn originally of two strands or plies, but now often used to indicate any fine yarn. It is used for baby's items and also for delicate, lacy knitted fabrics.

two-row buttonhole
Sometimes also called a cast-off or bound-off buttonhole. A buttonhole in

TWISTED ZIGZAG CHAIN STITCH

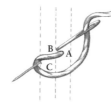 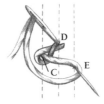

knitted fabric created over two rows. On the first row the number of stitches required for the length of buttonhole is cast/bound off; on the next row they are cast on again.

Two-sided Cross Stitch

In this variation of basic Cross Stitch, both sides of the fabric show the X-shape. Start by making a row of diagonal stitches spaced a complete stitch width apart, which means that the thread under the fabric will be diagonal, too. Then work back along the line completing the crosses, which will also complete alternate crosses on the reverse. To fill in the gaps on each side, repeat the whole sequence once more. *See also* Cross Stitch.

Two-sided Insertion Stitch

Unlike other versions of Insertion Stitch, this embroidery stitch is generally used as a decorative band rather than to join two pieces of fabric. It looks like a row of elongated stars from the front and a lattice from the back, so is reversible.

Two-sided Line/Stroke Stitch
See Double Running Stitch.

tying

(1) *quilting* A technique used in utility quilting, in which the layers of the quilt are held together with lengths of thread or ribbon threaded through and tied on the front. (2) *fabric* A dyeing technique, in which areas of the fabric are tightly bound then dipped into dye. The compressed areas do not take the dye, thus creating design shapes that can be very complex. *See also* batik.

U

underlap/underwrap
The edge of a garment that extends under another edge. *See also* overlap/ overwrap.

underlay
A strip of fabric under an area of the main fabric that needs reinforcing.

underlining
A lining used to add body to a garment, rather than to conceal seams and finish off the inside nicely. *See* lining.

understitching
Used to keep a facing/lining from rolling around onto the right side of a garment. After pressing the seam allowance and facing away from the garment, stitch through both a scant ⅛in (3mm) from the seam. You can also grade the seam allowance and facing/lining prior to stitching to eliminate bulk.

unravel
(1) *sewing* To separate or pull away threads from the cut edge of a fabric, or to fray the edge. (2) *knitting* To take the knitting off the needles and pull the yarn to remove rows already worked, either to correct a mistake or to pick up a dropped stitch.

upper arm measurement
Take this measurement just down from the shoulder, around the widest part of the arm.

utility quilting
Quilting with large and randomly sized stitches, so quilting can be completed more quickly than with fine hand quilting. Also covers techniques such as sashiko and tying. Also known as Big Stitch Quilting. *See also* Crow's Foot (quilting), Half Buttonhole, Mennonite Tack, Methodist Knot.

V

valleys

A term used in appliqué to denote a very sharp inward point, which is very difficult to stitch. *See also* peaks.

variegated yarn

Any yarn that has several colors in it, distributed randomly throughout the length.

Velcro®

A brand name for a type of fastening that comes in two parts; one half has tiny loops and the other tiny hooks so when pressed together they cling to each other. It is often used in children's clothing and shoes, and for items that need to be unfastened quickly.

velour

A mediumweight, closely woven fabric with a thick pile. It can be made using either a plain-weave or a satin-weave construction and it resembles velvet, but has a lower cut pile. End uses include apparel, upholstery and drapes.

VELVET STITCH

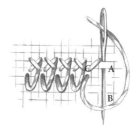

Velvet Stitch

An embroidery stitch used mainly in counted-thread work, and creates a pile effect on the front of the fabric. Work from left to right in rows, moving from the bottom upwards, creating rows of even loops that are cut and trimmed to the desired length at the end. If trimmed too short, the work will unravel.

velvet/velveteen

Velvet is a mediumweight cut-pile fabric in which the cut pile stands up very straight. It is woven using two sets of warp yarns; the extra set creates the pile. A luxurious fabric, it is often made with a filament fiber for high luster and smooth hand. Velveteen is a cotton cut-pile fabric, woven in the same way as velvet, with either a twill- or a plain-weave back.

vent

A lapped opening, usually in the hem at the back of a tailored jacket but sometimes in other garment sections.

vicuña

The yarn made from the very fine and lustrous undercoat of the vicuña, a relative of the llama, or the fabric made from this yarn. It is used mainly for outerwear garments. Vicuña is very expensive as the animal can only be shorn every three years, so it is usually mixed with wool. Imitation vicuña is usually made from sheep's wool.

view

Most patterns show different variations of the garments on the pattern package. Each variation is called a "view."

vinyl

A tough, smooth, flexible, non-woven, man-made fabric, often used where waterproofing is desirable—for example, for raincoats or hats. Fabrics can also be coated with vinyl to make them waterproof.

viscose

A man-made fiber made of cellulose from wood or cotton, and treated with sodium hydroxide. The resulting liquid can be extruded as a sheet (cellophane) or as a yarn (viscose rayon). *See also* rayon.

voile

(1) A crisp, lightweight, plain-weave cotton-like fabric, made with high-twist yarns. It is similar in appearance to organdy and organza and is used for blouses, dresses and curtains. (2) Voiles is also a general term used for semi-transparent curtains.

wadding

UK quilting term for batting. The middle layer of a quilt, lying between the top and the backing. It is traditionally made of cotton fibers or wool, and in antique quilts could be an old blanket or worn-out quilt. It is now generally a processed felted material that can be purchased pre-cut or by the length from a roll, and is normally cotton, polyester or a blend of the two. Wool and silk batting is available by special order.

waist measurement

Take the waist measurement around the natural waistline. If you have problems finding this, bend sideways: the crease that forms is the waistline.

waistband

A band at the waistline of a garment, which may have belt loops to hold a belt.

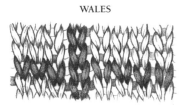

wales

The columns of stitches that run the length of a knitted fabric. *See also* rows.

warp

The threads or yarns that run lengthwise in woven fabric. Sometimes also called the floating threads/yarn.

waste canvas

This type of canvas has the threads held together by starch. It is laid over a non-evenweave fabric for counted thread work to be done. Afterwards, the canvas is dampened to remove the starch and the threads are extracted with tweezers.

waste knot
A method of securing threads with a knot on the top, which is cut off once the wool/thread has been sewn over.

water-erasable marker
A type of marker used in embroidery, quilting and any sewing project that makes a semi-permanent mark that can be erased with water. *See also* air-erasable marker.

water-soluble stabilizer
Water-soluble stabilizer is used in embroidery to hold the fabric firm while it is being worked. After completing the design, the stabilizer can be dissolved in warm water and removed. *See also* tear-away stabilizer.

WAVE STITCH

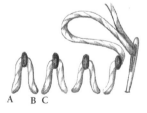

A   B C

Wave Stitch
An embroidery stitch that can be used to create a straight border of whatever width is needed, or worked in rows to fill an area. First work a row of small vertical stitches, then work across the row coming out below the vertical stitch, looping up, round and back down through the fabric again with a new thread. Subsequent rows loop in and out of the base of the previous row, so there is no need to repeat the vertical stitches; the thread only enters the fabric along the base of each looped stitch.

weave
Woven fabrics can be created with different patterns by using different sequences of warp and weft yarns. The most common weaves are: **plain**—also known as **tabby** or **linen** weave. This is the simplest and strongest weave, because it has single alternate warps and wefts; **basketweave**—constructed in the same way as plain weave, but with two yarns in each direction; **jacquard**—the warp is individually controlled with each pick passage, creating an intricate design; **leno**—a pair of warp threads pass over and under the weft yarns in a figure 8 or an hourglass twist, creating a geometric pattern; **pile**—woven with a second warp or weft thread, which forms loops or threads on the surface; **satin**—a weave that emphasizes a

continuous weft yarn, with as few and staggered warps as possible; **twill**—three yarns in one direction over two in the other, creating progressive steps to right or left; **twill herringbone**—a variation on the twill weave in which the direction of the twill alternates to produce a zigzag pattern, most commonly used for a type of tweed.

weaving

(1) *knitting* A technique in which the yarn not in use going across the back of the fabric in color work is twisted around the yarn in use, to hold it in place. If the spare yarn goes any distance it should be woven in every three stitches or so. *See also* stranding. (2) *fabric* a method of creating fabric by threading crosswise yarn over and under lengthwise yarn. *See also* warp, weft.

weft

The threads or yarns that run crosswise in woven fabric. Sometimes also called the filling yarn, filler, or woof.

weight

A term used to define yarn or fabric, traditionally based on its weight over a set area but now often used more generally to define the thickness of a yarn or how tightly woven and hard wearing a fabric is. Wadding/batting is still generally defined by weight—lightweight is around 1oz (30g), mediumweight is 2oz (60g) and heavyweight is around 4oz (125g).

welt

A method of covering the raw edges of a pocket or other opening. A single welt shows one band of fabric on the right side; a double welt shows two.

welt seam

A seam used in sewing, particularly to reduce bulk when working with heavy fabrics. From the right side it looks like a top-stitched seam. Stitch a plain seam and press the seam allowances to one side. Trim the under allowance to just under ¼in (6mm), then, on the right side, top stitch ¼in (6mm) from the

---

Knit Bit

During World War I, US President Woodrow Wilson allowed sheep to graze on the White House lawn. When the sheep were sheared, the wool was auctioned off and the proceeds were donated to the American Red Cross war relief fund.

seam, enclosing the trimmed seam allowance. For a double welt seam, edge stitch close to the seamline, as well; this will look like a flat fell seam on the right side.

WHEATEAR STITCH

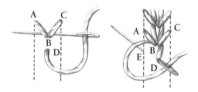

Wheatear Stitch

An embroidery stitch that is usually worked in a straight line, creating a spiky stitch like an ear of wheat. Draw two parallel lines before beginning and work downwards, making V-shaped stitches between Chain Stitches.

WHIP STITCH

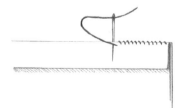

Whip stitch

A stitch in needlecraft used to hold two edges together, or to hold a facing in place by attaching it to a seam allowance. The needle is inserted from back to front, at right angles to the finished edges. The distance between stitches can vary, depending on the purpose of the stitch.

Whipped Backstitch

See Trailing Stitch.

Whipped Chain Stitch

A simple composite embroidery stitch that creates an attractive outline and can be worked in one or two colors. Make a line of Chain Stitch, then whip over and under each stitch, in a contrasting thread if required.

Whipped Running Stitch

See Cordonnet Stitch.

WHIPPED SATIN STITCH

Whipped Satin Stitch

An embroidery stitch used to add extra detail to narrow shapes. Work Satin Stitch to fill the shape, then whip the entire shape in a contrasting thread, working in diagonal lines spaced evenly a little apart.

Whipped Stem Stitch

A simple embroidery stitch used to create a heavy outline. Work around the shape in Stem Stitch, then use a contrasting thread to whip over and under each stitch without picking up the fabric.

whitework

A form of embroidery worked in white thread on a white background fabric. *See also* blackwork.

wholecloth quilt

A type of quilt with a single color top—often a single piece of fabric—usually quilted with a very intricate design. The interest comes from the patterns made by the stitching, rather than from pieced shapes or colours.

Windmill Crossing

A stitch in bobbin lacemaking, worked when two braids (a repetition of cross and twist) intersect. Treat each pair of threads as one thread and cross the center pairs, twist the right-hand pairs, put up a pin, and cross the center pairs again.

wool

Wool is the fiber or fabric made from the fleece of sheep or lamb. However, the term is also often applied to other animal hair fibers, including that of the camel, alpaca, llama, or vicuña.

work even

A term used in knitting and crochet patterns, often following a sequence of shaping with increases or decreases. You will have a different number of stitches than when you began that sequence, but you now carry on working over the number of stitches left on the needles.

Worm Stitch

See Bullion Stitch/Knot.

worsted

A firm-textured, compactly twisted yarn—originally wool—made from long staple fibers, or the fabric made from such yarn. The fibers are carded and made into continuous, untwisted strands, which are combed to make the fibers lie parallel and then tightly twisted and spun into yarn. The name derives from Worstead, a village in Norfolk, England. The term "worsted" is now used to refer to any yarn spun from fibers at least 3in (7.5cm) in length, or even to indicate a weight of yarn rather than a manufacturing process.

woven
See weaving.

WOVEN BARS

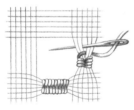

Woven Bars
A Hardanger embroidery stitch, which can also be used for drawn-thread embroidery. Withdraw an even number of threads and separate the loose threads into bars by weaving over and under until the threads are covered. *See also* Overcast Bars.

Wrapped/Whipped Bar Stitch
A stitch used in drawn-thread embroidery. To work the overcast bars, withdraw the number of threads required from the fabric and separate the loose threads into bars by overcasting firmly over these threads as many times as required to cover the group of threads completely. Also known as Overcast Bars.

wrong side
The wrong side is the side that will not be seen when a garment or accessory is in use; the right side is the opposite. With fabric lengths, the wrong side is often the side without a design—but there are some fabrics where the wrong side and the right side look identical. In these cases, stitchers can make their own decision—but fabric on a bolt is usually folded right sides together.

Y

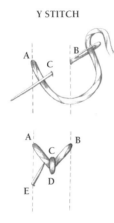

Y Stitch

A simple embroidery stitch that is also a basic part of many other stitches. Draw two parallel lines and work a stitch across them, bringing the point of the needle up again in the center to catch the loop of thread and pull it down into a V shape. Also known as Fly Stitch, Open Loop Stitch.

yardstick

A tool to measure lengths of fabric in yards or in parts of a yard. Most yardsticks are flat, wooden strips with black markings at regular intervals and metal tips. Many new yardsticks have imperial units on one side (three feet with inch and fractional inch marks) and metric units (one meter with centimeter and millimeter marks) on the reverse.

yardage

The length of yarn or fabric expressed in yards. Balls of yarn give the yardage on the ball band, spools of thread often have it marked on top of the spool. Pattern envelopes give the yardage of fabric required to make the garment in various widths of fabric, and often alternative amounts for fabric with and without a nap.

177

yarn
A twisted fiber used in knitting and crochet.

yarn over
A technique in knitting, which generally involves making a loop—or an extra stitch—over the needle, which at the same time creates a hole in the knitted fabric. It is an essential part of lace patterns and is generally abbreviated as yo. However, there are many variations on this—so always check the abbreviations given with the individual pattern. **Yarn forward** generally means bring the yarn over the needles, between two stitches; **yarn back** is the opposite.

yarn over hook
A basic movement in crochet, in which the yarn is taken over and around the hook before being pulled through a loop or loops.

yarn round hook
An alternative way of expressing yarn over hook in crochet.

yoke
Part of a garment that fits over the shoulders—which may be a separate piece of fabric to which the main part of the garment is attached, often in gathers or pleats.

Zigzag Coral Stitch

An embroidery stitch worked in the same way as Coral Stitch, but done by working each stitch diagonally across a pair of parallel lines to create a zigzag with a knot at each point.

zigzag hemming

A type of hemming stitch in which a row of small diagonal stitches is worked one way across the hem, then a second diagonal going the other way is worked on the way back, creating a zigzag catching the hem edge to the back of the fabric. It creates a very stable, firm hem, suitable for two edges that will be joined with Faggoting or one of its variations. *See also* fused hem, machine-rolled hem, rolled hem.

ZIGZAG CORAL STITCH

Zigzag Stitch

An embroidery stitch used for borders or to fill small areas, which looks like a row of Cross Stitches separated by vertical lines. It is worked in two passes, with the uprights and one direction of the diagonals worked first from left to right, and the opposing diagonals worked from right to left on the return.

zigzag stitches

Zigzag stitches are created on the sewing machine by adjusting the stitch width dial, so that the needle moves from side to side between stitches. The stitch length dictates if the zigzag will be open (for instance, to neaten a seam edge) or closely spaced (for instance, to stitch a buttonhole). Many modern machines have various types of zigzag as preset stitches for selection.

zip/zipper

Zip is the UK term, zipper the US. A zip is a pair of flexible strips of plastic or metal attached to tape, with interlocking teeth that are opened and closed with a sliding pull. *See also* separating zip/zipper.

ZIGZAG STITCH

SEWING PATTERN SYMBOLS

bust or hip point

buttonhole position—*the cross indicates the center point of the button*

dots/triangles/squares—*used to align pattern pieces along the seamlines, or to indicate design details*

fold line—*to be laid on a fold of the fabric. The fold line is not cut: the pattern piece is cut around the other sides*

lengthen/shorten lines

lining fabric

right side of fabric

seam line

cutting line—*on multi-size patterns, the cutting lines for different sizes are indicated by different line styles*

darts

grain line

interfacing

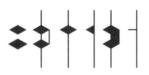

notches

pleat/gather points

wrong side of fabric

SYMBOL DESCRIPTION

 The washing process by machine or hand

 Chlorine bleaching

 Ironing

○ Dry-cleaning

 Tumble-drying (after washing)

✕ Do Not

WASHING

 Cotton wash (no bar) A bathtub without a bar indicates that normal (maximum) washing conditions may be used at the appropriate temperature.

 **Synthetics wash (single bar)** A single bar beneath the bathtub indicates reduced (medium) washing conditions at the appropriate temperature.

 Wool wash (double bar) A double underline beneath the bathtub indicates much reduced (minimum) washing conditions, and is designed specifically for machine washable wool products.

 Handwash only Do not machine-wash.

 Do not wash

BLEACHING

 Any bleach may be used.

 Only non-chlorine bleach may be used.

 Do not bleach.

DRY-CLEANING

 Must be dry-cleaned. Letter within the circle and/or bar beneath circle indicates to dry-cleaner the solvent and process to be used.

 Do not dry-clean

TUMBLE-DRYING

 May be tumble-dried at any heat setting.

 May be tumble-dried with low heat setting.

 May be tumble-dried with high heat setting.

 Do not tumble-dry.

IRONING

 Iron at low setting.

 Iron at high setting.

 Iron at medium setting.

 Do not iron.

KNITTING NEEDLE CONVERSIONS			KNITTING ABBREVIATIONS	
Metric (mm)	**US**	**UK/Canada (old)**	ABC etc	alternate colors as indicated in the color key
2	0	14		
2.25	1	13		
2.75	2	12	alt	alternate
3	-	11	approx	approximately
3.25	3	10	beg	begin/beginning
3.5	4	-	bet	between
3.75	5	9	CC	contrasting colour
4	6	8	C4B	cable 4 back
4.5	7	7	C4F	cable 4 front
5	8	6	cm	centimeter(s)
5.5	9	5	cn	cable needle
6	10	4	cont	continue
6.5	10 ½	3	dec	decrease/decreasing
7	-	2	DK	double knitting yarn
7.5	-	1		
8	11	0	dpn	double pointed needle(s)
9	13	00	foll	follow/following
10	15	000	g	gram
12	17	-	in	inch(es)
16	19	-	inc	increase/increasing
19	35	-	K/k	knit
25	50	-	k2tog	knit two stitches together
			k2tog tbl	knit two stitches together through back of loop
			kwise	knitwise
			LH	left hand
			LT	left twist
			m	meter(s)

MB	make bobble	st(s)	stitch(es)
MC	main color	St st	stockinette stitch
mm	millimeter(s)	tbl	through back loop
M1	make one stitch	tog	together
mult	multiple	WS	wrong side
oz	ounce(s)	wyib	with yarn in back
P/p	purl	wyif	with yarn in front
pat(s)	pattern(s)	yb	yarn back
pm	place marker	yd	yard(s)
pnso	pass next stitch over	yfrn	yarn forward and around needle
prev	previous		
psso	pass slipped stitch over	yfwd/yf	yarn forward
p2tog	purl 2 stitches together	yo	yarn over
		yon	yarn over needle
pwise	purlwise	yrn	yarn around needle
rem	remain/remaining	[ ]	work instructions within brackets as many times as directed
rep	repeat(s)		
rev St st	reverse Stockinette Stitch		
RH	right hand	*	repeat instructions following the asterisk as directed
RS	right side		
RT	right twist		
sk	skip	* **	repeat instructions between single and double asterisks as directed
SKP	slip one, knit one, pass slipped stitch over		
sk2p	slip 1, knit 2 together, pass slip stitch over the knit 2 together		
sl	slip		
sl-k	slip 1 knitwise		
sl-p	slip 1 purlwise		
ssk	slip, slip, knit		

CROCHET NEEDLE CONVERSIONS				CROCHET ABBREVIATIONS	
US size	**Metric (mm)**	**UK/Canada (old)**		ABC etc	alternate colors as indicated in the color key
14 steel	.60	-			
12 steel	.75	-			
10 steel	1.00	-		alt	alternate
6 steel	1.50	-		approx	approximately
5 steel	1.75	-		beg	begin/beginning
B/1	2.00	14		bet	between
B/1–C/2	2.25	13		blk	block
C/2	2.50	12		BP	back post
D/3	3.00	11		BPdc	back post double crochet
E/4	3.50	9		BPsc	back post single crochet
F/5	4.00	8		BPtr	back post triple crochet
G/6	4.50	7		CC	contrasting color
H/8	5.00	6		ch	chain stitch
I/9	5.50	5		ch sp/ch-sp	chain space
J/10	6.00	4		CL	cluster
-	6.50	3		cm	centimeter(s)
K/10½	7.00	2		cont	continue
L/12	8.00	0		dc	double crochet
M/13	9.00	00		dc2tog	double crochet 2 stitches together
N/15	10.00	000			
				dec	decrease/decreasing
Yarn conversions				DK	double knitting yarn
¾oz	20g			dtr	double treble crochet
⅞oz	25g			FL	front loop(s)
1oz	28g			foll	follow/following
1½oz	40g			g	gram
1¾oz	50g			hdc	half double crochet
2oz	60g			in	inch(es)

inc	increase/increasing	WS	wrong side
incl	include/including	yd(s)	yard(s)
lp(s)	loops	yo	yarn over
MC	main color	yoh	yarn over hook
mm	millimeter(s)	[ ]	work instructions within brackets as many times as directed
p	picot		
patt(s)	pattern(s)		
pc	popcorn	*	repeat the instructions following the single asterisk as directed
pm	place marker		
prev	previous		
rem	remain/remaining	* **	repeat instructions between single and double asterisks as directed
rep	repeat(s)		
rnd(s)	round(s)		
RS	right side		
sc	single crochet		
sc2tog	single crochet 2 stitches together		

US/UK terminology in Crochet and Knitting

		US	UK
sk	skip	single crochet	double crochet
Sl st	slip stitch	half double crochet	half treble
sp(s)	space(s)	double crochet	treble
st(s)	stitch(es)	triple/treble	double treble
tch	turning chain	double triple/treble quadruple	triple treble
Tdc	Tunisian double crochet		
tbl	through back loop		
tog	together	triple triple	treble
tr	treble crochet		Tunisian
trcl	triple cluster	basic Tunisian stitch	simple stitch
trtr	triple triple crochet	bind off	cast off
Ts	basic Tunisian stitch	skip	miss
Ttr	Tunisian treble crochet	gauge	tension

188

TATTING ABBREVIATIONS

Abbreviation	Symbol		
adj	adjacent	ss	switch shuttles
b	bead	st(s)	stitch(es)
beg	beginning	turn work	turn work over
betw	between	[ ]	work instructions
bp	beaded picot		within brackets as
ch	chain		many times as
cl	close ring		directed
dhs	double half-hitch set	*	repeat instructions
ds	double stitch		following the
dk	double knot/stitch		asterisk as directed
j	join		
lhk	Lark's Head Knot		
lp	long picot		
ls	lock stitch		
mp	medium length picot		
mr	mock ring		
number	number of stitches		
p	picot		
prev	previous		
rem	remaining		
rep	repeat		
rnd	round		
rw	reverse work		
r(s)	ring(s)		
sc	split chain		
scmr	self closing mock ring		
sep	separated		
sr	split ring		

MEASUREMENTS

1/16in (1.5mm)	7in (17.5cm)	20in (50cm)	35in (87.5cm)
1/8in (3mm)	7¼in (18cm)	20½in (51.5cm)	35½in (89cm)
3/16in (4.5mm)	7½in (19cm)		
¼in (6mm)	7¾in (19.5cm)	21in (52.5)	36in (90cm)
⅜in (8mm)		21½in (54cm)	36½in (91.5cm)
⅜in (9mm)	8in (20cm)		
7/16in (11mm)	8¼in (20.5cm)	22in (55cm)	37in (92.5cm)
½in (12mm)	8½in (21.5cm)	22½in (56.5cm)	37½in (94cm)
⅝in (15mm)	8¾in (22cm)	23in (57.5cm)	
⅝in (16mm)		23½in (59cm)	38in (95cm)
¾in (18mm)	9in (22.5cm)		38½in (96.5cm)
⅞in (21mm)	9¼in (23cm)	24in (60cm)	39in (97.5cm)
	9½in (24cm)	24½in (61.5cm)	39½in (99cm)
1in (2.5cm)	9¾in (24.5cm)		
1¼in (3cm)		25in (62.5cm)	40in (100cm)
1⅜in (3.5cm)	10in (25cm)	25½in (64cm)	40½in (101.5cm)
1½in (4cm)	10½in (26.5cm)		
1¾in (4.5cm)		26in (65cm)	41in (102.5cm)
	11ins (27.5cm)	26½in (66.5cm)	41½in (104cm)
2in (5cm)	11½in (29cm)		
2¼in (5.5cm)		27 in (67.5cm)	42in (105cm)
2⅜in (6.5cm)	12in (30cm)	27½in (69cm)	42½in (106.5cm)
2¾in (7cm)	12½in (31.5cm)		
		28in (70cm)	43in (107.5cm)
3in (7.5cm)	13in (32.5cm)	28½in (71.5cm)	43½in (109cm)
3¼in (8cm)	13½in (34cm)		
3½in (9cm)		29in (72.5cm)	44in (110cm)
3¾in (9.5cm)	14in (35cm)	29½in (74cm)	44½in (111.5cm)
	14½in (36.5cm)		
4in (10cm)		30 in (75cm)	45in (112.5cm)
4¼in (10.5cm)	15in (37.5)	30½in (76.5cm)	45½in (114cm)
4½in (11.5cm)	15½in (39cm)		
4¾in (12cm)		31in (77.5cm)	46in (115cm)
	16in (40cm)	31½in (79cm)	46½in (116.5cm)
5in (12.5cm)	16½in (41.5cm)		
5¼in (13cm)		32in (80cm)	47in (117.5cm)
5½in (14 cm)	17in (42.5cm)	32½in (81.5cm)	47½in (119cm)
5¾in (14.5cm)	17½in (44cm)		
		33in (82.5cm)	48in (120cm)
6in (15cm)	18in (45cm)	33½in (84cm)	48½in (121.5cm)
6¼in (15.5cm)	18½in (46.5cm)		
6½in (16.5cm)		34in (85cm)	49in (122.5cm)
6¾in (17cm)	19in (47.5cm)	34½in (86.5cm)	49½in (124cm)
	19½in (49cm)		

50in (125cm)	58in (145cm)	66in (165cm)	80in (200cm)
50½in (126.5cm)	58½in (146.5cm)	66½in (166.5cm)	81in (202.5cm)
			82in (205cm)
51in (127.5cm)	59in (147.5cm)	67in (167.5cm)	83in (207.5cm)
51½in (129cm)	59½in (149cm)	67½in (169cm)	84in (210cm)
			85in (212.5cm)
52in (130cm)	60in (150cm)	68in (170cm)	86in (215cm)
52½in (131.5cm)	60½in (151.5cm)	68½in (171.5cm)	87in (217.5)
			88in (220cm)
53in (132.5cm)	61in (152.5cm)	69in (172.5cm)	89in (222.5cm)
53½in (134cm)	61½in (154cm)	69½in (174cm)	
			90in (225cm)
54in (135cm)	62 in (155cm)	70in (175cm)	91in (227.5cm)
54½in (136.5cm)	62½in (156.5cm)	71in (177.5cm)	92in (230cm)
		72in (180cm)	93in (232.5cm)
55in (137.5cm)	63in (157.5cm)	73in (182.5cm)	94in (235cm)
55½in (139cm)	63½in (159cm)	74in (185cm)	95in (237.5cm)
		75in (187.5cm)	96in (240cm)
56in (140cm)	64in (160cm)	76in (190cm)	97in (242.5cm)
56½in (141.5cm)	64½in (161.5cm)	77in (192.5cm)	98in (245cm)
		78in (195cm)	99in (247.5cm)
57in (142.5cm)	65in (162.5cm)	79in (197.5cm)	
57½in (144cm)	65½in (164cm)		100in (250cm)

Acknowledgements

For my Dad, who always thought anything was possible.

Special thanks to Nana and my Mum, who taught me how to sew and knit and so much more, and to Michael, Maria and Pob, who kept the children entertained while I had my head down working.

With thanks to Katie Cowan and Michelle Lo for commissioning this book, Lotte Oldfield for her great illustrations, Ben Cracknell for the design, and Sarah Hoggett and Katie Hudson for their thorough editing.